THE ADVENTURER'S GUIDE TO WALT DISNEY WORLD

BY: COLLIN KENDALL

LEGAL INFORMATION

WHAT'S INSIDE?

4 Introduction

6 Beginning the "Journey"

7 Your Home Away From Home

      8 Deluxe Resorts

      16 Moderate Resorts

      25 Value Resorts

      30 Deluxe Villas

34 Creating The Impossible

      35 Magic Kingdom

      72 Epcot

      104 Hollywood Studios

      126 Animal Kingdom

155 Your Highway In The Sky!

159 The Disney Dining Plan

163 Fastpass+: A Developing Idea

165 Final Thoughts

167 Special Thanks

INTRODUCTION

Disney is full of stories and stories are really what make each day of our lives special and uniquely different from the day before. Some of us go to work, others to school, but each of our lives tell a story. The Disney parks are no different. Each attraction, dining location, and resort tells a unique tale. However, the stories that you can't see are the ones that make a Disney vacation so special. As strange as that may sound, the reality is that when you go to Disney, it isn't about the place, it's more about the people. We're all there to share an experience with our friends and family, creating memories that will last a lifetime. The parks are changing, but what will always stay the same is the feelings that the parks create. We're all drawn to Disney for a different reason, but you can't help but notice there's just something different about the parks. There's a factor at Disney that sparks a feeling of nostalgia. You can walk into the parks with a big smile on your face and just remember all the wonderful memories of life. The memories don't even have to be from Disney. I can guarantee that one way or another you'll have a moment where everything just seems to make sense. Every Disney enthusiast knows that feeling. It's like being a 6 year old kid again without a worry in the world. That's really what it's all about. Don't worry about doing absolutely everything, just enjoy everything you do. The simplest of moments can create memories that will last a lifetime!

WHY WRITE A GUIDE TO WALT DISNEY WORLD?

I knew I wanted to write a book about Disney, but the hard part was finding something that hadn't been done before. At first I thought about questions I had heard in the parks and came to a realization. Nobody has ever created a straightforward, helpful, flip through guide to Disney World. The Disney guide books that do exist are all WAY too big to actually take to the parks where the guests need them the most. So, that is exactly what I have in store for this book.

Guests wander through the parks asking cast members questions that are incredibly easy to answer, but most of the time are overlooked in books. "The Adventurer's Guide to Walt Disney World" aims to answer those questions before you have to ask them, but can also be used as a tool within the parks. Say, for example, you have an elderly family member. It's your first time at Disney and you have no idea what kind of attraction awaits you at the end of each queue line. Instead of wasting all that time in line or asking every single cast member what each attraction is like, take out the guide and flip to the attraction you have a question about. Almost every experience will have a description of what it's like and any warnings I may have for the attraction. I truly believe you can find an infinite number of uses for this book throughout the parks and resorts. Hectic vacations develop from confusion, and the best cure for confusion is a book full of answers!

SO WHAT'S WITH THE TITLE?

When it came to naming the book, I was a bit lost to be completely honest. So I thought, "What is the one thing I want people to know after reading this book?" What I came up with surprisingly made sense, "The Adventurer's Guide to Walt Disney World". When I broke it down, I realized why it came to mind in the first place.

The Adventurer's Club was a part of what was formally known as Downtown Disney and, more specifically, Pleasure Island. The club was dearly loved by many guests, but I never got to experience it due to my age and it's disappointing closure many years ago. Despite not seeing it for myself, the name made sense with the theme of the book. I wanted to write a book that provided facts based on my experience, but also explained to people the reality in the fact that you can never see and do everything at Walt Disney World. Anyone who has been there will reluctantly tell you this, but it is something we have to learn to deal with as Disney enthusiasts.

Even though this concept seems disappointing, it actually just gives every Disney geek and average guest alike a reason to return to the parks and have a new and unique experience each and every time. The parks are always changing and that is something that must be taken into consideration while I am writing this book and as you, the reader, are looking through it. Feel free to read through and explore the book cover to cover or jump to the topic you have a question about. Hopefully every aspect of this "handbook" will help you in making decisions on where to eat, what to ride, and where to stay, along with answering any questions you may have regarding the many aspects of Walt Disney World. And with that, we will begin our journey through the Disney World parks and resorts.

BEGINNING THE "JOURNEY"

A plan, no matter how elaborate or minimalistic, is essential to a great trip to Walt Disney World. Certain elements have to be planned to enjoy the experience to the fullest possible extent. These things include: dining reservations, fastpass+ (which has its own section), resort accommodations, monorails, and even the attractions themselves. With everything to consider, the process can seem incredibly tedious and off putting to many guests. That realization itself is why I compare planning to a journey.

The planning is part of the fun. I know we've all heard the old adage that getting there is half the fun and in no means is this what I am referring to. Quite the opposite actually. The "journey" is one that every Disney fanatic understands. The excitement that builds up, the anticipation of a new experience, the food you're going to enjoy, and last but not least, the memories that you will inevitably create.

As your plan develops, you have to keep one thing in mind that many Disney guests often overlook. You cannot see and do everything at Walt Disney World. I know that is not what you want to hear, and no guest ever wants to hear those words. When I tell people this, I always get a similar response. Something to the extent of, "I am going to pay all of this money to go to Disney and you tell me I won't be able to see it all!" My simple answer always has to be yes.

If you take absolutely every detail of this book and analyze and plan until you think you have the ultimate plan for your vacation to do and see absolutely everything, you still won't see it all. To be honest, you would be missing the point of the book completely. You must plan for the Disney parks in a way that is unique from all other vacation destinations. You must prioritize what you want to do the most and leave out the things you could pass on doing. That is the essential key to this journey. Use this book, take it with you to the parks, read it before your vacation, but above all, use it to make the absolute most of your experience. In all reality, it could truly be a life-changing vacation. So, without further ado, lets jump right into it and help you plan your experience of a lifetime.

YOUR HOME AWAY FROM HOME

When planning your vacation to the parks, there are a variety of choices for all types of budgets, but one mistake that almost all guests consider. Everyone considers the ever present draw away from the Walt Disney World resorts to the resorts located off of the Disney property. In my humble opinion, this is one of the biggest mistakes you can make in regards to your overall travel experience. There is something unique about experiencing that "Disney Bubble" atmosphere. In other words, that feeling you get when Disney takes care of everything. For those of you completely new to Disney, when staying at a Walt Disney World Resort, they take care of all transportation to and from the parks, to and from the airport (through the Magical Express system), and even go to the extent of allowing you to park (for free) and leave your car if you never wish to use it during your vacation. Lastly, as a resort guest you even have the opportunity to park for free at all of the Disney parks if you choose to drive to your destination. While staying on property, you have the opportunity to enter the parks before everyone else as a part of extra magic hours that are exclusively offered to resort guests on select dates and times.

As you can see, the benefits of these resort accommodations are astounding. These benefits are what many of the hotel chains near property can't possibly provide. The costs of each element that Disney provides outweighs any cost difference the off property hotel creates. The benefits of "saving" that money, even potentially, isn't worth the drastically lower quality experience either. Each Disney property has unique and incredible levels of theming that you definitely don't want to miss.

Before we get to the individual resorts, I should first point out that there are four levels or classifications of resorts. Disney labels these resorts by their price and level of luxury. The Deluxe resort category is the highest quality available on Disney property followed by the Moderates, and then the Values. So, with those ideas in mind, let's find your perfect home away from home.

DELUXE RESORTS

-Above: Disney's Boardwalk Resort

Disney' Animal Kingdom Lodge

What is it like?: This resort in particular is one of the most unique experiences you can find in a Disney resort. The resort itself is based on the idea of essentially living in a lodge that immerses you in the African Savannah in a unique and original way. The lodge is home to well decorated, African inspired guest rooms that truly immerse you in the feeling of the African Culture and create an experience that cannot be matched anywhere in the world. The adventure truly comes alive through the animals found at your backdoor roaming in their simulated natural habitats. If you purchase certain rooms, you can even be at eye level with the giraffes from your very own balcony. The resort itself is breathtaking and I cannot recommend it enough to those who appreciate various cultures and want a unique experience that encompasses all aspects of a Deluxe resort. There is unique theming elements, incredible restaurants, and surprisingly, Animal Kingdom Lodge is consistently one of the more budget-friendly Deluxe resorts.

The Downside: The resort itself is the farthest from every park, except its neighbor, Disney's Animal Kingdom. The second closest parks are Epcot and Hollywood Studios at about a 15 minute bus ride away. Magic Kingdom, however, is 20-25 minutes away on a good day.

The Best Fit: People who will enjoy this resort the most are animal lovers and those who are willing to be a good distance away from most parks, despite paying a premium price for accommodations. The distance from most of the parks is probably part of the reason for the lower price point while still being a Deluxe tier resort.

Disney's Beach Club Resort

What is it Like?: The resort itself is a part of arguably the best location on the Disney property. A short boat ride or walk away from both Epcot and Hollywood Studios lies this quaint little group of resorts. The group includes the Yacht and Beach Club along with the Boardwalk resort. The Beach Club, in particular, is part of a two resort hotel set up. It's brother, in a way, is the Yacht Club which has a similar feel and theme, but is also unique in many ways. The Beach Club has a beachfront hotel atmosphere that feels as if it was pulled right out of what many believe to be a sort of early Florida influence. The atmosphere is very homey for many guests and is unique in the fact that it is the location of the second largest pool on Disney property, which it shares with the Yacht Club. The enormous pool is the main draw to the resort and is partially sand-bottomed, making it very fun for children to enjoy. It even features an enormous slide that stems from a ship out by the lagoon on which the resort borders.

The Downside: Despite its many exemplary features, a downside could be the sand-bottomed pool itself. Many guests find it unique and clever, but many also find it a bit strange to get used to and it's definitely something to know when entering the booking process.

The Best Fit: This resort is definitely for a wide variety of guests. The pool is great for children, but the atmosphere lends itself to unique and incredible restaurants steps from your resort and many within your resort. Dining at the Yacht and Beach Club features everything from the ultra upscale Yachtsman Steakhouse to the much more casual Beaches and Cream, near the pool. Also worth noting is that the Beach Club offers villas in addition to standard rooms which are much larger. The larger space accommodates more guests, but is also much more expensive. However, if you split up the cost among more guests it is usually cheaper to keep a larger group together utilizing the villa option rather then buying multiple standard rooms.

Disney's Boardwalk Inn

What is it like?: Across the water from the last resort mentioned, lies questionably the best themed and most highly overlooked resorts on the Disney property. The resort itself, is a lakefront boardwalk that includes the various aspects of the boardwalks across the United States and of the past. It has almost a carnival aspect to it, complete with live entertainment and other features, but in a very upscale way. It is very tasteful and entertaining as a place to stay. The pool, for example, is based around a coney island style wooden rollercoaster slide that winds and twists then dumps you out into the main pool area. If you're not a fan of the water, take to the boardwalk itself, steps from your hotel room door for a ride on a Surrey bike, a drink at the ESPN club, a dance at Jelly Rolls, or even a meal at one of the many high class and family friendly restaurants. Each location is complete with a stunning view of Epcot and the surrounding resorts. Once you finish off your night at the parks or on the boardwalk, go to your resort and take in the luxury that is found throughout your uniquely themed room, which tastefully elaborates upon the previously mentioned themes.

The Downside: For this particular resort, a downside is very difficult to come up with. The only negative there could be is that there is constant entertainment into the early hours of the morning at the waterfront boardwalk itself. At Jelly Rolls in particular, which is a dueling piano bar, the music continues well into the night and could potentially disturb a few guests. Thankfully, a vast majority of the guest rooms are not near this location and even the ones that are, the music would be very difficult to hear from within the guest rooms.

The Best Fit: You could put basically any type of guest into this resort and they would have an exceptional vacation due to the varied experiences available and the prime location for accessing any of the parks. The price is a bit high, but as with any resort, book your accommodations early and you can save a significant amount of money.

Secret: While it isn't necessarily condoned or recommended by Disney, one of the more entertaining things to do at the Boardwalk is to race the Surrey bikes. Surrey bikes are offered by Disney and a few other resorts nation wide, but the bikes are actually four to six person bikes that are built in a similar fashion to a golf cart. The bikes are pedaled just like any other bike, but you have one person who drives in the front row, while everyone pedals. Small children can be put in a smaller seat in front of the driver, so everyone in the family can be included no matter if they can reach the pedals.

Even though riding the Surrey bikes is fun by itself, when you get two families or groups of any sort together you can have even more fun with a friendly race. This is the part Disney probably doesn't appreciate, but is an absolute blast to watch and probably just as fun to do. Some groups have started racing the bikes around the lake. You start at the bridge right before Epcot side by side then race down the hill, around the corner, in front of the Yacht and Beach Club, make the turn by the bridge to the Swan and Dolphin, and finish when you cross under the Boardwalk sign. You almost have to stop racing there because if you don't there will be too many people to do so safely. Be careful, have fun, use the Yacht and Beach Club side of the lake, and ring the bell as loud as you can. You can't help but laugh watching it and it's fairly safe sense everyone will hear you coming!

Disney's Contemporary Resort and Bay Lake Tower

What is it like?: This resort is the most normal resort on property, but also one of the most extraordinary, for all of the right reasons. It is fairly similar to most modern hotels today, but unique in many regards. The largest being it's location and design. The location is the best possible for accessing and viewing the Magic Kingdom. It is without a doubt the only resort that you can literally walk to the Magic Kingdom from and view the entire park 24/7 from your balcony. The rooms are familiar to anyone who stays in high quality hotels, but uniquely Disney through certain touches throughout the room. The unique nature of this resort comes from outside of your rooms door. The Disney Monorail system runs right through the building and functions as transportation to the Magic Kingdom and Epcot Center parks with ease by way of the Grand Concourse Station.

Next door and connected by a bridge, lies the newest addition to the Walt Disney World Resort family, Bay Lake Tower. The tower is home to many upscale rooms, many of which lie directly behind Space Mountain, overlooking Tomorrowland. It is an incredible edition to the Contemporary that blows guests away by its level of luxury and varied room types and experiences. Unfortunately, a majority of the rooms are reserved for Disney Vacation Club. But, if you are a Vacation Club member, be sure to look into the Top of the World Lounge. It is exclusive to Vacation Club members and offers an incredible view for the Magic Kingdom fireworks.

The Downside: The Contemporary is the farthest possible distance of a Disney Resort from the Animal Kingdom. However, that is a small price to pay to be able to potentially view the Wishes nighttime fireworks spectacular from your balcony. There is even a balcony in the Grand Canyon Concourse available to all guests to watch the nighttime fireworks, complete with the music you would hear within the parks. However, it is also one of the most expensive resorts on property which, at peak times, can reach astronomical nightly rates.

The Best Fit: As by far the closest resort to the Magic Kingdom and with the ease of transportation through the monorail system, this is the ultimate one-stop shop to please any guest if your budget can stand it. It can appeal to any guest through it's many features, but particularly suits those who want to be in the Magic Kingdom as much as they possibly can throughout their vacation.

Secret: While not necessarily hidden, the design of the resort has a unique story. The resort was built by sliding each individual room into the frame of the larger building. The design concept never really caught on, but the idea itself is pretty neat. The building idea was actually used in a similar manner one other time for the Polynesian Village Resort.

Disney's Grand Floridian Resort

What is it like?: The Grand Floridian is widely known as the most high end resort on the Disney property, complete with multiple upscale dining experiences and retail locations. The resort's theme is elaborate, but fits a certain audience drawn to it's style. When you enter the lobby, you are greeted with a step back in time to a classy waterfront resort, complete with floor to ceiling white, elaborate, decorations which bring a feeling of being in the classy hotel of your dreams. The rooms are no exception to this feeling and give you an experience that you can never forget through the Victorian styling that carries over from the lobby and common areas. One of the main draws to the Grand Floridian for many guest is the ease of transportation to the parks with monorail access to both Magic Kingdom and Epcot. In addition, the Grand Floridian offers a beach front viewing location for the Wishes nighttime fireworks spectacular at Magic Kingdom, directly across the Seven Seas Lagoon.

As an added bonus, accompanied by an enormous price tag, the pinnacle of luxury Disney has to offer can be found at this resort. For example, various boats and even yachts can be rented and used for a romantic dinner or other special events, accompanied by a host to serve you. Also, the Grand Floridian contains the highest quality restaurant on all of the Disney property. Many have voted it the best restaurant experience in all of Florida. Of course, this restaurant is none other than Victoria and Albert's, a culinary experience like no other, complete with a multiple course meal fit for a king and catered to your individual preferences.

The Downside: As result of the theme, many parents feel as if their children cannot be themselves and have unrestricted fun times at the Grand Floridian. However, this is not the case and children are encouraged to stay, but the atmosphere does tend to come off as a little stuffy and overly fancy for some guests liking.

The Best Fit: The Grand Floridian is definitely for those with a large budget and desire for the ultimate luxury that can be had on the Disney property. Also, if you book at the right time and avoid peak season for the parks (usually spring break, summer, and New Years) you can sometimes catch a much cheaper rate at this Deluxe level resort.

Disney's Polynesian Village Resort

What is it like?: As you walk in the main entrance, you are immediately embraced in the culture and styling of the Polynesian influence. As the most recently redesigned resort, the property is in excellent shape and home to some of the largest rooms of all the resorts. The theme itself is a favorite among guests young and old. You can sit back, relax, close your eyes, and feel as if you're steps away from the ocean on a tropical island. The atmosphere truly embraces the guest and even goes as far as to gift each guest with a Hawaiian Lei upon check in and any time you enter the resort. The design itself lends your experience to becoming one that is incredibly magical and something you will not soon forget. The accommodations are no exception to the trend the lobby sets for the resort. The rooms are unique and perfectly balanced between theming and functionality. The theme is subtle but extraordinarily well done. As a bonus, the Polynesian Village has many Polynesian influenced restaurants, a bar that is an experience in and of itself named Trader Sam's Grog Grotto, and even a luau many nights of the week.

The Downside: The Polynesian Village Resort is probably the hardest resort to find a flaw in. It has a prime location, also on the monorail line to the Magic Kingdom, and a well developed, enveloping theme. The only potential downsides are that some guests will be disappointed in the changes that have been made to the resort during the updates, but overall most people leave extremely pleased with their stay.

The Best Fit: The resort itself is possibly the best resort to have two vacations in one. You can experience that vibe that you get from a beach resort, but also enjoy all that Disney has to offer. As for specific guests, the resort is perfect for all ages and desires and is complete with virtually anything a guest could want.

Secret: It is widely accepted that this resort is the place where the Beetles band officially broke up. While in town as a guest, the paperwork was sent to John Lennon in his room at the Polynesian around the time of the opening of the Magic Kingdom. The details of the break up where listed in the paperwork and John Lennon signed it on site.

Disney's Wilderness Lodge

What is it like?: Upon entering the lodge you are embraced by the most spectacular lobby your mind could ever imagine. From floor to ceiling, there are totem poles and a wooden design that pleases nearly every eye. The overwhelming theme is that of a lodge that would be found in the Northwestern United States at the turn of the century national parks. It is even complete with an erupting geyser. However, if you are not a fan of the great outdoors, do not be alarmed. In my opinion, this is the most welcoming resort on property and one in which you will want to take time just to explore with any extra time you can find during your vacation. The excitement that builds from the experience here is hard to put into words.

The Wilderness Lodge is stunning and looks like a beautiful, grand scale cabin, tucked away on the corner of the same lake that borders the Magic Kingdom. There are boat rides to that park as well, as a form of transportation. In the lodge itself, the rooms are spacious and inviting, even going to the extent of offering bunkbeds for kids for no extra charge. However, the real draw to this resort for my family and I has always been the resorts' nighttime presence. The property comes alive at night through offerings of campfire S'mores on the beach and the atmosphere that seems to envelope you after the sun goes down. It truly feels as if you're deep in the forest, miles away from any big city lights or sounds, and it can be truly astonishing.

The Downside: Despite being a Deluxe resort, and bearing the same price tag, there are only two types of transportation. One being a boat to the Magic Kingdom, Contemporary, and Fort Wilderness Campground, and the other being buses to the rest of the parks. For a similar price you could have the option of boat, bus, or monorail at the Contemporary, Polynesian Village, and Grand Floridian.

The Best Fit: The encompassing nature of this resort makes it perfect for families looking to spend time away from all the hustle and bustle of daily life and really connect with each other in a way that is indescribable. There is just something about the resort that brings people closer together and I have had the opportunity to experience it first hand. Even with the elaborate atmosphere, this is actually one of the Deluxe resorts that can have a fairly reasonable price point if you book early enough. In regard to Disney resorts though, early is actually almost half a year in advance!

Secret: It's not really a secret, but often something overlooked. If you take the short walk over to the villas, there is a room devoted to the obsession that Walt Disney himself had with steam trains like the ones found in the Magic Kingdom. The room even includes two cars from the original Carolwood Pacific Railroad, a small scale, rideable, train set that was built and maintained by Walt Disney in his very own backyard! It's great to see the influence such a simple passion of Walt Disney had to help develop the parks into what they have become over the years.

Disney's Yacht Club Resort

What is it like?: The Yacht Club is very similar to the Beach Club Resort mentioned earlier with one key difference. The resort focuses more on the nautical aspects found in the overall theme. The Yacht Club is upscale, but not quite to the extent of the Grand Floridian. The upscale aspects are very subtle, but the influence is noticeable. The afore mentioned Yachtsman Steakhouse finds it's home here at the Yacht Club. As the theming enters the rooms themselves it is very subtle like the rest of the property, but very comfortable. Nothing is off-putting or in your face about the design, but as the more upscale of the before mention, adjacent property, it plays its part well and the theme helps better develop the resort overall.

I cannot forget to mention the views of both Epcot and the magnificent lights of the Boardwalk just steps from your door on a dock style walkway to Epcot. The lights are spectacular as they reflect off the water late at night or on an early morning walk to your destination. Boat transportation is also available to both Epcot and Hollywood Studios that is usually quite nice. Epcot is about a 5-10 minute walk so it's probably better to just walk, especially from The Beach Club. While you can walk to Hollywood Studios as well, I definitely wouldn't recommend it unless staying at the Boardwalk across the lake. There is a walkway, but it takes a boat about 20 minutes to get there and the walk takes much longer. Also, by the time you get there, your feet will probably hurt before you even get to the park, and nobody wants that.

The Downside: As a Deluxe resort, it has many loving fans, especially in the world of Vacation Club, but when compared to the elaborate themes found at other Deluxe resorts, this one often pales in comparison. The theme is just not for everyone, but it's proximity to the parks is outstanding. The transportation can be a little strange too. For any of the resorts with boat transportation, the boat will not run during strong thunderstorms or lightning scenarios for obvious reasons. Sometimes that causes issues for the guests at Hollywood Studios in particular. If the boats aren't running, you have three options: 1. Disney will eventually send a bus. 2. Wait for the storm to pass and the boats to resume. 3. Make the long trek through the rain along the walking path back to the resort. You will get soaked, but it is an option if you're short on time. All of the resorts with boats operate with the same rules, so that isn't necessarily only for this resort, but is definitely something to keep in mind.

The Best Fit: The best fit here is anyone who loves to be at or near the Epcot park any time of the day. By accessing a back entrance into the World Showcase, guests at the Boardwalk, and Yacht and Beach Club have premier access to the park and ease of entrance nearly any time of day. Epcot is literally steps from your door.

As you can see, this is not intended to be an in depth overview of the Deluxe resorts, but more of a guide of what to expect and many facts that guests often never consider. However, these Deluxe accommodations come with a high price tag usually starting at upwards of $400+ per night of your stay and peaking at the most crowded times of the year at an astonishing $1000+ per night. If the financial reality of these resorts does not cause a problem, I cannot recommend this tier high enough. For those who are not willing or able to spend this type of money on a vacation, do not be turned off by the idea of a Disney vacation. The Disney property is home to many other resorts. With that, we will move on to a lower price level alternative found in the Moderate tier resorts that are just as uniquely themed as those of the Deluxe resorts, but are often simply set up in a slightly different way.

MODERATE RESORTS

Now I have to take a second to clarify. The Moderate resorts are a step down in overall quality when compared to any Deluxe resort, but are still, in my opinion, miles ahead of many standard hotels across the nation. Contrary to more mainstream resorts and those mentioned above in the Deluxe category, the Moderate level Disney Resorts begin to become much more spread out. In nearly every case, a Moderate resort consists of many buildings and many different areas sprawled across a rather large piece of land. This type of development requires a separate check in area and lobby setup in one building, while the guest rooms, food court, and pool, are on another part of the property. The various buildings that make up the larger resort are never all connected and have outdoor entrances.

Now with all of this under consideration, many guests still prefer some of the Moderate resorts over the Deluxe resorts for various reasons. The most central being the elaborate and enveloping themes that span a much greater area of the property when compared to the higher tier. As the theming is spread out over a greater area of land, the resort experience becomes quite immersive. For most guests though, the single greatest selling factor is that the various Moderates have a much more affordable price tag with very few accommodation sacrifices. With that information out of the way, we'll get right to it, starting off with the Caribbean Beach Resort.

Disney's Caribbean Beach Resort

What is it Like?: When you arrive at Caribbean Beach, you are treated by a variety of colors and multiple buildings sprawled across a beautiful lake. At check in, you will be assigned an island of the Caribbean of which your hotel room location and building is named after. If you are lucky or pay the additional fees, you can be placed at buildings of your choice and you can even make requests at check in if rooms are available (maps of the property are readily available online). The resort itself is very spread out and, as a result, if you do not get a room near the pool and food court area, you could be walking a good distance to either of these amenities. However, the walk is very enjoyable and well themed in a Caribbean style complete with tropical foliage and a variety of colors.

Caribbean Beach is set apart from some of the other Moderate resorts by the presence of secondary pools at each "island" in addition to the main, themed, resort pool. As a result, you have a variety of options and even have the opportunity to rent (for an additional fee) small speed boats to ride around the lake that are exclusive to resorts with bodies of water. The rooms themselves are fairly simple, but very colorful, complete with bedding featuring tropical fish, Caribbean inspired furniture, and decorations. Fairly recently, there has been the addition of pirate rooms at Caribbean Beach. The separately themed rooms are complete with a ship shaped bed and mast for a headboard. The rest of the decorations follow suit as well. Even the tables and nightstands immerse you in the pirate theme reminiscent of the Pirates of the Caribbean attraction which was developed into the movies we all know and love.

The Downside: You are going to notice a significant increase in transportation time utilizing the buses. Each section of the resort has it's own bus stop, but the same bus stops at every bus stop. So unless your stop is near the middle of the route, you have to either stop at all of the other stops leaving the resort or coming back from the parks. For those late nights and early mornings in the parks, and for those that get carsick, this is not always the ideal transportation situation. Again, I will mention that if you can find your way around the property, you can always drive your own vehicle and park for free as a resort guest at any park you choose to visit. If you do, try not to rely exclusively on a GPS device. The mapping for the Disney property as a whole is fairly poor since it is always

17

changing and GPS units usually just make getting around harder than it needs to be. In most cases, it is better just to pay attention to the Disney signs that are all over the roads and they will direct you to certain parks and resorts across the Disney property.

The Best Fit: For those worried about money, this is often times the most cost effective Moderate resort. That being said, it is a great place for the beginning Disney parks goer who has not experienced the different transportation offerings. You will never compare your travel time to other means of transportation and will have a fonder appreciation of the transportation overall. It is a great place for kids, especially with the option of pirate themed rooms and is a good fit for anyone looking to just enjoy their stay and the benefit of a much more cost effective vacation.

Disney's Coronado Springs Resort

What is it Like?: As you enter this resort, you are immediately encompassed into an atmosphere that is undoubtedly influenced by authentic Hispanic culture. It is a very unique resort and features queen beds opposed to the doubles that are found in many non Deluxe level resorts. The design itself is very elaborate, but correct in relation to its theming influences. The colors are very similar to how you would picture the streets of Mexico in your mind and potentially how they would look in that country or that part of the world in general.

The atmosphere, as a result, is very vibrant and it carries over to the outdoor pool area. The main pool is unique and elaborately themed with a pyramid inspired waterfall that flows down into the pool below. As far as the rooms are concerned, the theme is carried over from the resort as a whole, but in a very subtle way. The patterns and decorations across the standard rooms are similar to the overall design influences, but is not as in your face as you would expect from the outside looking in. However, Coronado Springs is also home to various business conferences due to being a Disney property that contains a convention center. Some people may find it worth noting that Coronado Springs may have more than just resort guests calling it their home for the week. Sometimes, it's a little hard to get in the Disney spirit when there are dressed up business people walking around your resort all the time.

The Downside: The downside is really not too bad for this resort, but more of an inconvenience. With the exception of Animal Kingdom Lodge, this is the farthest resort from the Magic Kingdom. The other side of that issue is that it is the closest resort to the Animal Kingdom at the Moderate level and is very close to the Blizzard Beach Waterpark. Depending on what you prefer, this could be a great location either way.

The Best Fit: For those individuals who are not concerned with transportation issues to Magic Kingdom, and would rather have a larger bed (Coronado has queen size beds) than a shorter ride, this is the perfect option. Also, anyone needing more space for conference style accommodations should really appreciate the amenities of Coronado Springs. The resort offers suites and junior suites in addition to the standard rooms which are great for larger families or groups. These specific suite style rooms do have a higher cost as well, which may not work for every budget.

The Cabins at Disney's Fort Wilderness Resort

What is it Like?: Fort Wilderness is different from all the other resorts. Now, I have alluded to the fact that many resorts are "unique" for various reasons, but Fort Wilderness is not similar to any other resorts except through theming. The wilderness influence is similar to Wilderness Lodge, but the set up of the campgrounds is very different. The Fort Wilderness Cabins are part of the Fort Wilderness Campground and share a similar set up to the RV camp sites that cover a majority of the area. The cabins themselves are great options for larger families and those who really love the great outdoors. It's really the only place on property that isn't surrounded by big buildings and it creates a much more friendly and welcoming environment. It's almost like a small town of RV's and cabins. The cabins in particular are similar in size to a mobile home, but a little larger, nicer, and definitely more permanent. This type of accommodation includes an oven, stove, and even a fairly large refrigerator. Outside of your cabin, you even have your own deck complete with a picnic table if you wish to enjoy the beautiful Florida weather while eating a "home-made" meal.

Not in the mood to cook after a long day in the parks, or just need a break from them? Take the short ride or walk over to the common area by the lake and enjoy a meal at Trails End, which features a southern style buffet each night and full service menu for lunch. If you're looking for an even more exciting family adventure, try and get a reservation for Mickey's Backyard Barbecue and get ready for a show that you won't soon forget. Even if these options don't sound like your cup of tea, there is a variety of various activities found steps from your cabin door. The property is complete with a horse barn, a canoeing adventure, and even a bike trail through the woods. So no matter what your preference, there is always something fun to do at the Fort Wilderness Cabins. You don't even have to stay there to partake in the activities on property, so you may want to go look around if any of that sounds like fun. Most of the activities require an additional fee, but are very cheap entertainment that is enjoyable but simple, just like a real camping trip!

The Downside: Fort Wilderness, due to being a campground mostly, and the cabins being a later add on to the property, is very spread out. Depending on your location, the common area can be a fairly decent walk. However, many experienced guests rent or bring golf carts with them. There is bus transportation but it has multiple stops before heading to the parks unless you choose to go to the Magic Kingdom. The Magic Kingdom has its own boat transportation dock near the common area which you can reach by riding an internal shuttle around the resort or by other means of transportation. To be completely honest, if you're going to Epcot, you're probably better off just riding the resort boat to the Contemporary then taking the monorail transportation to Epcot. The resort boat is a great way to resort hop as well if you're looking to spend some time eating at or exploring other resorts. The boat goes to Wilderness Lodge and the Contemporary, but by utilizing the monorail, you can get to Magic Kingdom, the Grand Floridian, and the Polynesian Village resort.

The Best Fit: The cabins are a great fit for large families or those who don't necessarily want to eat every meal in the parks. You can make your favorite recipe, and have a great night lounging on your own porch, creating priceless memories with your friends or family. Keep in mind, the additional space comes with a slightly higher price tag that is comparative to a Deluxe resort or suite style room at Coronado Springs. The extra money, however, can be overcome if need be by having the ability to cook your own meals while on vacation.

Secret: Early on in Disney history, the first Disney water park was created steps away from the common area of this resort. Later, it was abandoned due to a potential micro organism that was supposedly found in the lake that the water park was attached to and part of the attractions ended in. Other possible explanations exist for its closing, but due to similar organisms found in other Florida lakes recently, this could be a likely explanation. To this day, if you ask a cast member about River Country, the name of the park, many will deny its existence (despite being viewable by the public to an extent) or come up with another explanation for the area. However, please do not attempt to explore River Country today as it is fenced off to the public and is rumored to have significant consequences for anyone who has done so. My advice would be to view River Country from the boat to Magic Kingdom when you are traveling from Wilderness Lodge to Fort Wilderness where it will be on the edge of the lake on the right hand side of the boat. As many rumors have developed, it's surprising that Disney has never done anything with River Country, but to this day it still exists and is virtually untouched!

Disney's Port Orleans Resort-Riverside

What is it Like?: As you drive onto the property this resort encompasses, you can't help but notice the New Orleans influence in the theming. That being said, Port Orleans encompasses two resorts that are nearly always listed separately on various websites, including Disney's reservation site. They also carry varying prices and those prices fluctuate, but on average, Riverside is often more expensive on a nightly basis. Each of the two areas included on the property have the same general theme of New Orleans influence, but differ drastically in the details.

The first, and often preferred by many guests, is Riverside. As you walk around, you are presented with more of the nature aspect of the New Orleans theme. The buildings are scattered but not quite to the extent of some of the other Moderate style resorts. This section of Port Orleans is also home to the larger of the two lobby areas(there is one for each section) and the larger foodcourt and pool area. Both the food court and the sit down restaurant have a unique setting that encompasses the riverside dock theming.

The expansive theming is the main draw to the Riverside resort, in my opinion. As you leave the lobby, you step out onto a dock that doubles as a small, rentable watercraft area to ride on the river as well as a transportation location to Disney Springs via pontoon boat. The New Orleans influence is quite beautiful and many of the room locations across the property take on the uniquely Louisiana style of columned mansions, complete with beautiful gardens and water views. The overlying experience is truly encompassing, complete with a real river that runs right through the property and continues on to Disney Springs. The river itself is an incredible part of the resort experience. It winds over to the French Quarter section of the resort then on through the Saratoga Springs Tree House Villas on a leisurely journey to your destination.

Port Orleans is my go to resort for those looking to save some money, but who also want to have a more upscale Disney vacation experience. The elements that make up the theme are quite possibly some of the most beautiful on Disney property and the resort has a great location. Port Orleans is fairly close to every park except Animal Kingdom, which is about 15-20 minutes away. Contrary to the other Moderate resorts, Port Orleans has fewer bus stops within the resort. This aspect by itself was a huge factor for my family when we stayed at the resort and it saved us quite a bit of time, especially early in the morning. It's always great to be able to jump on a bus, hit a couple bus stops (instead of five or six) and be on your way to your final destination.

The Downside: The only real downside to Riverside is that there are a select few rooms that are quite a ways away from the main areas and bus stops, but the walk is always enjoyable due to the elaborate scenery.

The Best Fit: Anyone who wants a luxury experience at a modest budget and appreciates the beauty in the small aspects of an experience will truly appreciate all this resort has to offer. Also, with the creative pool design that is fairly large and complete with fountains that the whole family can enjoy, this is a must consider resort. As if that isn't enough, there are "Royal Rooms" available at the resort which are similar in size to all other rooms but have a drastically different theme. The beds have incorporated lighting affects that mesmerize and features of the rooms themselves make you have the feeling of staying in Cinderella's castle. Royal rooms are sure to please any princess fan or just someone looking for something unique to enjoy during their vacation.

Disney's Port Orleans Resort- French Quarter

What is it Like?: The overall idea of the broad resort is mentioned above, but this particular section of the French Quarter is exactly as it sounds. It is a great representation of the French Quarter and exhibits a wonderful influence from that section of New Orleans. From personal experience, this is my go-to Moderate when I get the opportunity to visit the area. As soon as you walk onto the property, you feel as if you're right in the heart of the best part on New Orleans. The streets are indistinguishable from the real deal. You could even take a picture and send it to a friend or family member of one of the "streets" that the rooms sit on and they would completely believe you had changed your vacation spot or got really lost on your way to Florida!

French Quarter is very quaint for a Moderate resort. The property is the least spread out of all of the Moderate resorts, especially when focusing on French Quarter itself. The lobby is small but elaborate. The majority of the lobby area is a glass walled open air feeling area that encompasses the unique French influence of the property. As you enter, there is a beautiful fountain in the french style, but the real immersing factor comes from the nearly always present live jazz music of Scat Catt's Club found just across the hall. Beyond the lobby is a food court area, which both Riverside and French Quarter have present, and a gift shop that is simple, small, but very useful for necessity food items, in addition to souvenirs.

Once you leave the lobby, the resort becomes even more alive with a main pool complete with a serpent themed slide and alligator characters unique to the resort area. French Quarter also has its own smaller boat launch to both Disney Springs and Riverside. Once you get past the main areas, the rooms themselves are unique in that most have large windows to the outside of the room, often viewing a garden or pool area upon request or reservation preference. The theming of the rooms is subtle, but has various dark wood detailing which creates an upscale feel. As a perk to the resort, the beds are queen size opposed to the doubles which are found at some of the Moderate tier. All things considered, this resort is one that I find to be the most accommodating and the best deal for the money on Disney property. So, book your vacation here and prepare to sit back and relax in New Orleans style along the Sassagoula River!

The Downside: Certain times of year, this resort is significantly more expensive per night than similar offerings in the category, such as Caribbean Beach. That being said, the quality of resort for the extra money is hard to overlook. Even though the cost can be more, the experience really is worth the money. The only way to describe this place is that it's classic, but timeless. It seems as if every time you come here, you can expect it to be just as you left it. I know I said that the parks are always changing, and largely for the better, but it's always nice to have a place that stays the same. Sometimes, if something isn't broke, don't fix it, and Disney seems to realize that occasionally. Port Orleans doesn't need to change. The theming is near perfect, the experience is worth every penny, and the value is better than just about any resort. It's a place you can always count on to produce good memories and is probably my number one recommendation when taking cost into perspective. Yes, it is a little more expensive than some, but I would never doubt that it is worth the money.

The Best Fit: The resort is possibly best for those who want to have a vacation that can be leisure and excitement all in one. You don't have to go to the parks every day to have a great time due to the various offerings and low crowd level found at the property. Additionally, you are a twenty-minute boat ride from the constantly developing and expanding Disney Springs, which is completely free to visit. So, if you just want a nice place to stay and relax, this is your resort. I stayed at French Quarter for a week on one particular occasion and went to the parks for only two days and really enjoyed my vacation despite the little time spent in the parks. It was a wonderful change to not go 24/7 and I was able to explore and enjoy the many aspects of the resort experience I often don't have time to look into. However, if you're into the commando style Disney experience, going 24/7, this resort accommodates you as well. You really can't go wrong here if the price is right for your budget!

Now before we move onto the final group of resorts, a way too often published stigma about this tier has arisen and needs to be addressed. Many Disney enthusiasts will tell you that if you're going to go to Disney World, don't go if you can only stay at a Value resort. You should stay off property if this is all you can afford. Those claims could not be farther from the truth, in my humble opinion. The Value resorts have their place just like the rest of the resort tiers.

As a result of many of these claims, families look past Disney World and move on to a beach or other vacation destination. A Disney vacation should never be viewed by the level of resort you're staying in or how luxurious your room is, but rather focussed on the true goal of the vacation destination. Walt's goal was to build a place where families could come and have fun together, leaving the troubles of the world behind. The Disneyland project in and of itself in California was based on an idea that Walt developed while sitting on a bench watching his daughter have fun at an amusement park. As a result of the conditions and dilapidated state he observed around him, Walt realized that he could do better and a better experience was ultimately made. Some people may not agree, but in my opinion, Disneyland was the test. The real plan Walt must have had as a visionary, would have to be for something far larger in scale and concept than Disneyland itself. He had to want to go on to a grander scale and that was exactly what he had planned later on.

The development of that idea is what we now experience as Disney World in Florida. However, the vision is still the same. It is a place that families can come and leave the world behind and just be with their families in a place full of people having the time of their lives. So, the Disney magic is still in the small details of these Value resorts, but the ultimate draw to Disney isn't luxury per say, but rather the opportunity to be with friends or family and enjoy the parks. To create memories and an experience that will last a lifetime. So, if anyone questions your decision to stay at a Value resort, in reality you should be questioning their purpose in going to Walt Disney World in the first place. We're all having the same experiences in the parks and creating memories which has been the ultimate goal from the beginning. With that, lets get right into it and explore Disney's Value resorts.

VALUE RESORTS

A Value resort is essentially a standard hotel room you would find anywhere else in the world. They are similar to a Hyatt or Hilton of sorts, but the differences that are present, in the theming, is something that cannot be explained fully on paper. The design elements at these resorts are more elaborate and obvious than at any of the other resort tiers. From the hundred foot replicas of your favorite characters, to a life size football field, one of these is sure to spark your interest in the vacation planning process.

The resorts themselves are laid out in various ways. For example, the All-Star sub sections of the Values are spread out through various buildings within a larger complex. Each building group is based on a category such as sports, movies, or music. Each of these three properties are near Hollywood Studios and Epcot, but also near Blizzard Beach and Animal Kingdom. The transportation from each is all by bus to the various parks and Magic Kingdom is by far the greatest distance away at a near 20-25 minute journey.

The other layouts for the two remaining Value resorts not previously mentioned are similar in design, but different in location. The Art of Animation Resort, the newest on property, sits across a small lake from Pop Century. This area is directly behind Caribbean Beach and Hollywood Studios. The resorts are a little closer to Hollywood Studios and Epcot, but farther away from Animal Kingdom. However, the ride to Magic Kingdom is fairly close to that of Animal Kingdom due to the centralized location.

The Value category rooms by themselves are very different in nature to the before mentioned resort tiers. The Values are a lot less subtle in their theming and lend themselves to a different Disney experience that many enjoy and also many do not. As a result, book these resorts with a different experience in mind, but don't let that alarm you. The Values are still like no other resort you have stayed at or will probably ever stay at again. The experience is different for sure, but the overwhelming benefits of staying on Disney property and witnessing all the parks and resorts have to offer is still an experience that you and your family will remember for years to come. With those small cautions out of the way, lets get right into what all these properties have to offer.

Disney's All-Star Resorts

What is it Like?: Each of these resorts fall into a category due to the fact that this title of "All-Star Resort" encompasses 3 different properties with three different themes. So, as a result, this section is broken up into an overall category for the resort group then separated into the sub sections for each theme the title encompasses.

Overall: The All-Star resorts are each unique, but cover a variety of potential audiences. The rooms all have outdoor entrances, and are very similar in layout and square footage. As the bottom tier of resorts, these hotels, in my opinion, fall into the lowest level of service and quality of the Disney resorts. However, the price reflects the difference on a nightly basis and is largely worth it to many guests in order to spend more time in the parks or extend their vacation timeframe. The lower cost can often lead to a longer stay! Other guests choose these resorts from an economic standpoint and who can blame them. The benefits of the price point make up for the less luxurious experience, but still offer fun, clean, budget conscious accommodations for any Disney parks guest.

Music Resort: This All-Star is probably the most minimalistic in theming out of all the Disney resorts. The theming is obvious, but the least elaborate of the Value tier. Each wing has a music based theme encompassing everything from The Three Caballeros to a larger than life juke box. The main pool is very large, but the resort also accommodates many guests, so the pools can become quite crowded as with any Value resort. The good news is that there are also other smaller pools throughout the property. Other amenities include many quick service dining options by way of a food court. The rooms are straight forward: 2 double beds, a tv, and a small table, which is basically all you would need. The Music Resort also offers family suites that are much larger and include a living room area which doubles as additional sleeping arrangements for up to six total guests. Overall, if this theme works for your group, it is a great option to give you a hotel like experience with the elaborate theming found at all of the Disney resorts.

Sports Resort: The Sports Resort is very similar to the Music Resort in the way of room set up and accommodations, but differs in a few ways. One being that sports does not offer the suite rooms found at the music resort. The suite rooms are only available at the Pop Century and Music Resorts in the Value tier. Second, it differs greatly in theming. The sports section is fairly obvious in theming based around various sports, but the creation of that concept is quite creative. The resort is covered with larger than life sports objects and fields that can actually be used for "recreation".

That aspect is positive for some guests and not for others. Due to it's close proximity to the ESPN Wide World of Sports complex, the resort is often filled with sports teams participating in various events across the property. For this type of guest, the sports theming is a perfect fit. There is plenty of room for small scale sports practices or just a family who likes to throw some football to get away from the parks for a few minutes and enjoy their resort (something I personally recommend to all resort guests: explore, enjoy, and take advantage of all your resort has to offer). While considering the All-Star Sports Resort, it's very hard to overlook that it also has a very large, themed pool, secondary pools, and a food court complete with many quick service dining options. Even though there are some great benefits to the resort, always be prepared to be surrounded by teams attending athletic functions throughout your stay.

Movies Resort: Being the last of the All-Stars listed, Movies is my personal favorite due to the theming and the overall Disney based environment. Movies is the only All-Star resort that focuses on the Disney films directly. There is just something about a 100+ foot Woody from Toy Story that makes you feel immersed in the Disney magic. Other than Toy Story, many other movies are featured that can fit a variety of audiences and age groups including everything from Fantasia to The Mighty Ducks. As for the pools, the larger of the two pools features Sorcerer Mickey on what is built to look like a stage production in front of the pool. The second pool is based on a hockey rink which is themed around The Mighty Ducks film series. As for the rooms, they are the same standard rooms found in all of the All-Star resorts and strike a balance between functional and immersive. Overall, this is probably your best option when considering the three All-Stars.

The Downside: Besides lacking luxury found in the higher tiered Disney offerings, the largest draw back to the All-Star resorts is the massive amounts of resort guests. The buses are often very crowded as a result of the groups that usually travel together and are probably the largest draw back to the lower price point. Recently, this situation has became much less of an issue due to the new Disney buses put into service which are double the length of a standard bus and serve almost exclusively the Value resorts.

The Best Fit: The All-Stars are the best fit for anyone who is not too picky or expecting the pinnacle of luxury during their vacation. If your goal is to save a large sum of money, this is your resort! It is very budget friendly and offers several services which off-property resorts will not in the same capacity as Disney does.

Something to Consider: In regards to the pool crowd situations, remember that as an All-Star resort guest you are allowed to use any of the All-Star resort pools, even if you are not staying in that particular area. For example, you can use a movie pool if you're staying at the sports resort. Recently Disney has been cracking down on this "pool hopping" practice at some of the Deluxe resorts by requiring Magic Bands for pool entrance. However, I do not believe that will ever apply to this resort and there is no speculation of this at the time of writing this guide. Scanning Magic Bands for pool entry started at the Deluxe resorts recently and could potentially trickle down in time.

Disney's Art of Animation Resort

What is it Like?: As the latest and greatest of the Value resorts, Art of Animation is very different than the other Disney resorts. As a result of being the newest addition to the Disney resort family, the set up is unique and has many features Disney has recognized other resorts lack. So, that being said, Art of Animation is separated into 4 sections, each having a theme based on one of the Disney animated movies: Finding Nemo, Lion King, Cars, or The Little Mermaid.

The Cars section has a pool featuring the Cozy Cone Motel from the movie and the Finding Nemo section features what Imagineering has termed the Big Blue pool. Each of these pools are very expansive and offer a variety of things for the whole family to enjoy. If the atmosphere isn't enough, while you are actually swimming in the Big Blue pool, it comes alive even under the water with sounds from the movie Finding Nemo. This is something that is very hard to explain, but incredibly entertaining in person. In addition to the theming, the resort differs from other Value resorts in quality as well. It is still spread out, just as the others are, but the rooms themselves feel as if they are a much higher quality experience and are a much more creative design.

In conjunction with the standard rooms, suite rooms are also available at the resort that sleep up to 6 guests and contain a small kitchenette area. The kitchenette features a microwave as well as a sink and small refrigerator. A design element unique to suites is that in select rooms, the table in the kitchenette area doubles as a fold down bed for an additional guest sleeping arrangement. In regards to dining, Art of Animation features one of the best food courts on property, and some guests even find a way to visit the resort just to experience the gift shop and food court even though they are not staying at the property. For a while, this was common practice at all of the resorts. People would go and visit other resorts just to see what they were like or to eat someplace new. Recently Disney has tested a system of paid parking for non resort guests, which could potentially eliminate that opportunity. Many guests are very unhappy about the potential of having to pay to visit other resorts, but no one knows for sure if it will ever become a permanent reality.

The Downside: All of these extras found at Art of Animation come with an additional cost which is very similar to that of the Moderate tier resorts or worse. However, the majority of the rooms are suite rooms so the price is even higher for those accommodations. The suite price gets very near that of a Deluxe resort during certain times of the year. It's a little disappointing to see a Deluxe tier price point from a location with only bus transportation.

The Best Fit: Despite the pricey nature of the resort, it is a must consider property for any family going to Walt Disney World. It creates a great atmosphere and the theming is based around the movies many are considering to be the second "Golden Age" of Disney. You can't really go wrong at this resort with the exception of the fact that transportation is all by bus and can be fairly tough at times. With that being said, larger families will find this to be one of their best options before having to move into the Deluxe Villa or Moderate suite price range.

Disney's Pop Century Resort

What is it Like?: While the Art of Animation Resort is the newest resort, Pop Century is probably the best value for the money. While only being standard rooms, Pop Century has benefits that many of the other resorts in this tier do not. The first of those differences comes in the way of location. Pop Century is the only Value resort who's busses aren't always overcrowded. The Art of Animation's bus situation is quite similar but has a much higher nightly price point. Pop century is also the only Value that shares the same property area as the Art of Animation Resort and is just a bridge away from all that brand new resort has to offer.

As the name implies, Pop Century's theming is based on pop culture across the various decades. Each decade has a section of the overall resort from the 50's into the late 90's. That design created three distinctly themed pools. The first and largest is the Hippy Dippy pool which is considered the main pool of the resort. This Hippy Dippy pool is shaped as a very large flower, complete with water sprayers for the kids and since this is Disney, the kids at heart as well. In addition, there are two other pools considered quiet pools of sorts and feature a large bowling pin and computer monitor shape. All of the pools are very uniquely themed as with any Disney resort, but these, as well as the bus situation, really sets this Value resort apart from the others in the category.

Pop Century also has a very large food court complete with a variety of options that can accommodate virtually any guest preferences. As for the resort rooms themselves, they are simple on the inside with Disney touches by way of a Mickey Mouse comforter and some themed wall art. The extensive theming seems to stop at the resort room door. Pop Century offers a fairly standard hotel room experience, which is one of very few on property.

The Downside: There is nothing too special about the rooms themselves, but for those who don't worry too much about being really embraced by the theming, this will not be a problem. The resort can be fairly crowded, like all of the Value Resorts, but it is much better than the All-Stars for a very similar price.

The Best Fit: If your budget falls into the Value category, this is most likely your best option when taking into consideration transportation, crowd level, and overall experience. The price is comparable to the All-Stars, but has many of the benefits of the usually higher priced Art of Animation. If you are not too worried about extensive in-room theming, this would be a great resort option that can fit nearly any budget.

As we wrap up this tier of resorts, there is only one level truly left and it is the best of the best that the Disney company has to offer. However, there is a reason I saved it for last. I mentioned at the end of the Moderate level that Disney World was an extension of Walt Disney's overall vision of a place that families can have fun together. So, by putting these two resort tiers next to each other, I intend to create a point that many Disney resort guests often overlook or choose not to except for one reason or another.

The issue is ultimately entitlement. Some people may disagree, but I am beginning to see it more and more in the parks. Many resort guests exhibit the notion that since they are paying more money they should get "more" out of their vacation. The idea bleeds over into the parks every day. Your first trip, you may not notice it, but if you look for it, it becomes blatantly obvious. Some people seem to think that since they are paying to be there, they are all that matters in the parks. Don't get me wrong, not all guests are this way, and many will go out of their way to make the experience great for everyone. However, I bring this up for a reason. By "buying into" a resort tier, don't expect a different in-parks experience. The parks are great for everyone and ultimately the whole point of Disney World was to be able to enjoy time with your friends and family. That is the best part of the experience and whatever you do and wherever you choose to stay, don't let that purpose slip away. That being said, this next resort tier is the pinnacle of luxury and is the ultimate way to experience Disney if your budget allows.

DISNEY'S DELUXE VILLA RESORTS

When attempting to find a room at the Disney resorts and money is no issue at all, consider the Deluxe Villas. As I mentioned before, these rooms offer no difference to the guest experience in the parks themselves, but are ultimately an addition to your overall Disney experience.

The Deluxe Villas are actually sections of the Deluxe resorts and offer the same general theming, but often with a different level of service. Villas, in many cases, on the Disney property, offer much larger rooms. These villas can sleep up to 8 or more guests in a few cases and are basically a home away from home. Usually, the villas are reserved for Disney Vacation Club members, but Disney offers a select amount of rooms throughout all parts of the year for other guests to purchase for the week. As a Vacation Club member, you would use a points system to book your resort similar to a time share program. Since the rooms are designed with Vacation Club "owners" in mind, they are very expensive and only fit the most extensive budgets. At peek times, many of these rooms can cost well over $1,000 per night and can even reach much higher prices based on resort and room type. The Vacation Club is basically a very expensive time share program, but you are offered some very luxurious accommodations as a result of the money you are spending to be a member. If you're interested in the program, start as early on in your Disney vacations as you can. The longer you are a member, the more you get out of your money in the long run. It's a great program for staying at the villas and is the most price efficient way to book the higher priced rooms.

As for the most unique offerings of the villas, look no further then the grand villas available at many of the Deluxe level resorts. These villas are hard to describe in any other word than incredible. Many are available in 2 story options and can accommodate up to 12 guests. They are the largest rooms on property and feature the best the resorts have to offer. The best of the best in my opinion are the largest villas at Bay Lake Tower, Animal Kingdom Lodge, and the Treehouse Villas of Saratoga Springs.

Saratoga Springs itself fits into a unique category that includes itself and the Old Key West Resort. These resorts are ultimately Disney's Vacation Club Resorts. They are separated from the Deluxe and Deluxe Villas by the fact that these resort rooms are reserved for Vacation Club members more exclusively to a certain extent. Very few rooms are available to the general public, but they seem to be getting increasingly more available as the resorts get older and newer villas are being developed. Of course, as always, this is just my opinion based on personal travel experience. However, it is obvious that the Vacation Club must be growing because villas are being added to nearly all of the Deluxe resorts.

The two nearly exclusive resorts themselves are fairly spread out, but very nice and offer a somewhat quiet experience. That being said and due to their limited availability to non-Vacation Club guests, I will only mention them briefly below:

Disney's Old Key West Resort: Located near Disney Springs and a short distance from Magic Kingdom lies this unique resort. A village type atmosphere of multiple buildings and a unique sand castle themed pool gives the resort a very beach centered feel. The rooms are very large and cater to larger families or those who like to spread out a little. Old Key West has a group of followers that very few Disney resorts have. Many guests in the Vacation Club stay exclusively at this resort and love that it is one of the lesser known resorts. For years I didn't even know where the resort was located until I went and played golf at Saratoga Springs, which is the adjacent property.

Disney's Saratoga Springs Resort: This offering is very strange as far as accommodations go. Until you get into the larger one and two bedroom villas, the only offering is a studio room that features a queen size bed and double size sleeper sofa. The strange accommodations don't always work for all guest types. In addition to the rooms, the resort layout is quite different than the others. Saratoga Springs has the feel of a small village or town complete with Disney's Lake Buena Vista golf course club house on the property (Disney's most difficult golf course). In addition to these features, the resort is in very close proximity to Disney Springs.

So, getting back to the villas themselves, found at both of the resorts just mentioned, my ultimate villa pick would be the Treehouse Villas at Saratoga Springs. This will probably surprise some Disney enthusiasts because of the fact that the Bay Lake Tower villas are so close to the Magic Kingdom and the Treehouse Villas only have one means of transportation, which is by bus. In my opinion, this is what makes this villa option so great. It is exclusive, separated, and incredibly unique. The Treehouse Villas are 3 bedroom villas that are individually built in the woods along the Sassagoula River that runs past the Port Orleans Resorts and ends at Disney Springs. The villas are beautiful and give your family or friends plenty of room to spread out. Despite these great features, the villas are not the newest on property, but still one of my favorites. Also, the set up is somewhat similar to the much higher priced waterfront Bungalows at Disney's Polynesian Resort.

These Bungalows are the newest addition to the Polynesian Village and sit on the edge of the lake directly across from the Magic Kingdom Park. You can see the castle from your balcony and even watch the fireworks from your very own plunge pool (basically a cold hot-tub). The bungalows are the highest quality accommodations available through Disney Parks and Resorts and are very limited in availability as a result of their only being 20 total. The price per night starts at well over $2,000.

As you can see, these villas are the ultimate in luxury accommodations and their price reflects it. As a result of their price tag, and exclusive clientele, I won't spend any more time on these very large villas. The other villas are actually fairly reasonable in comparison, and many offer a studio style room which are very similar to a Deluxe level standard room. The theming is nearly the same, but the set up of the rooms are slightly different and often feature a queen or king size bed and some form of rollout for additional guests. The price of these studios are still very high and offer no real advantage over standard Deluxe tier rooms. The studio rooms are basically special accommodations for Disney Vacation Club Members, just like the villas.

After analyzing all types and levels of resort accommodations Disney has to offer, hopefully you have a better idea of what is available and aren't too overwhelmed. Believe it or not, there is much more information available about each of these resorts, but my goal was to provide a few facts that Disney may not always tell you. You usually have to learn many of these things by trial and error and hopefully you now have a good idea of the best fit for you and your family or friends needs. So, with the accommodations out of the way, let's get to the part you probably got this book for in the first place, the attractions themselves.

CREATING THE IMPOSSIBLE

The goal of attractions in Walt Disney's mind seemed to be largely based on innovation and defying what many people thought to be impossible. Today, the Imagineers (Disney's form of various specialized Engineers) continue that legacy and continue to evolve and create the future through attractions that everyone can enjoy.

However, some attractions are best fit for certain guests and certain guests are best fit for certain attractions. That will be the main goal of this section: describe the rides, their intensity levels, and their history, giving each and every guest something to take with them to the park to supplement their park maps. The maps give locations, but virtually no descriptions of the rides themselves. Ultimately, this will save each and every guest time and effort during their stay and even grow their Disney knowledge, no matter if they are a veteran Disney goer or a first time visitor. All the while, I will try and preserve the magic that the Imagineers have worked so tirelessly to create.

In addition to the attractions, dining opportunities will also be included in a similar way. Each in-park dining option will be listed within the area it can be found. Hopefully, this will help each guest preparing for their vacation to find a dining location which fits their "plan of attack" in touring the parks or simply helps them find what's close by, in order to save time in the parks. Extra time is always a great resource and you can never get enough of it!

Many of the dining locations require reservations that can be booked up to six months in advance. Often, first time guests do not utilize the dining offerings, especially the sit down type of reservations, due to price and availability, but it is possibly my favorite part of the Disney experience. The food at nearly all dining locations is incredible and, in many cases, an experience that you do not want to miss. There is everything available on property from high end luxury to character meal buffets to simple sit down dining. There is something for everybody to enjoy and dining is something you should never overlook, unless your budget ultimately cannot handle the additional cost of the meals themselves or the Disney Dining Plan (this has its own section later in the book).

An additional reason dining is included in this section is that the dining locations themselves, can be viewed as attractions. They are themed in many cases and have a story to tell just like all of the attractions on property. With those few things being said, lets go ahead and begin our journey through the parks, an adventure that you will never forget!

DISNEY'S MAGIC KINGDOM

-Above: Main Street Station

MAIN STREET, U.S.A.: It's the easiest part to get to and the most overlooked part of the Disney experience. Every guest enters and leaves on this street, but for many, they view it as nothing more than an oversized gift shop. For me, it is much more and it should be so for each and every guest. Walt Disney designed this street after one of his many childhood home towns, this particular one being Marceline, Missouri. In the design, it is believed that forced perspective was used to make the street appear much larger than it actually is, as well as the castle in the distance. The result of this design is an entrance that immerses the guest, but is also full of hidden secrets and experiences nearly every first time parks goer will overlook. For me, the street is an attraction due to the atmosphere itself, but a few slightly lesser known facts make it one of the best, wait free, experiences in all of the parks.

The first of these details is the extensive level of theming. You can meet the mayor, visit the train station for a ride, read the windows that often hold elaborate backstories, and of course, be sure to pick up and listen to any antique telephone that you may find. One holds a funny conversation you may not want to miss on the other end of the phone. As for the windows, you could write books about them alone and I'm sure someone has. Each window has a backstory and every name listed has a much greater one. I know what you're thinking, "I doubt I'll have time to look at windows and I'm not going to waste my time on that." You're probably right, but if you have a few extra minutes while waiting on a parade to start or a fireworks show, be sure to look around and maybe even flag down a cast member to ask a few questions. I'm sure they'll know about the windows or be able to find you someone who will. With the street itself covered, we'll move onto each and every attraction of the Magic Kingdom that have warmed the hearts of guests for generations.

Main Street Station- As the first attraction that you come to in the Magic Kingdom, the train station and trains themselves leave an impression on every guest. From their involvement in the opening celebration, to their role as an attraction, they can be enjoyed by every guest that enters the park. The trains are a staple for Disney that will never and should never be changed. Contrary to popular belief, one of the steam engines found on the tracks each day is actually the oldest running attraction in the Magic Kingdom. Many believe that Prince Charming Regal Carrousel is the oldest attraction in the park and it may be by some definitions of "attraction", but ultimately one of the trains, before its restoration, is actually slightly older.

The steam trains were imported from the Yucatan Peninsula after being ran for several years and then abandoned. The Disney Company came in and bought three trains, one being older than the rest, and sent them to be restored with intricate detail. The original build date for the oldest locomotive was 1916 and Prince Charming Regal Carrousel was originally built exactly one year later. The result is the oldest attraction in the park, but it is truly remarkable that both attractions and all of the steam trains were built nearly 40 years before the park even opened in 1971.

Town Square Theatre- Once everyone gets into the park, at some point or another, they want to see Mickey Mouse and his friends. This location is the only place in the park to see the mouse himself. As a result, the wait times at the Town Square Theatre can be quiet long. One tip that will save you a lot of time is to go before or after one of the the parades or fireworks shows. The wait time is virtually non-existent at these times and you get to spend much more time with the characters as an added bonus. Let's be completely honest, who doesn't want to get their picture with Mickey Mouse at Walt Disney World?

Tony's Town Square Restaurant- For years, this was a hidden gem at Walt Disney World, but after a few menu changes, it is not nearly as good as it once was. That being said, the atmosphere is very pleasant and has a Lady and the Tramp theming that is very creative, but also very subtle within the restaurant. The food itself is Italian cuisine, as the name suggests. It's decent food at best, but I personally believe it used to be much better. Unfortunately, that seems to be the common consensus among guests more recently. Very few patrons experience a meal that is worth the price in any regard. Fortunately, a couple of things do make up for it to a certain extent.

The greatest benefit of this dining option is that it is a sit down dining location in the Magic Kingdom that is not too terribly hard to get a reservation for and not overly expensive in comparison to the others. For example, on a family vacation on New Years Eve, largely considered the most crowded day of the year, we were forced to drop a reservation at a resort based restaurant due to a tip from security that the park would be closing due to capacity very soon. Basically, if we left the park, it would be a one person in one person out situation as a result of fire codes. Long story short, we were offered a reservation at Tony's by guest services on the busiest day of the year. Now, this may not always be the case, but it can never hurt to go to the restaurant in the morning and ask for a walk up reservation.

Main Street Bakery- A great option for a breakfast or even just a fun snack is this bakery. Formally, the location offered many pastry items, but recently was transformed into a Starbuck's coffee location that also carries many pastry-type items. So, that turned into a win-win situation for everyone, despite the many opinions about Starbucks in the parks. But, we won't get into that. This is a walk-up style counter, just like any other Starbucks, but with many additional options. However, it does not offer every Starbucks drink found in the ordinary corporate stores.

Plaza Ice Cream Parlor- Now who doesn't love a good old-fashion ice cream shop? That is exactly what this location is. Complete with the old-style counters and open ice cream topping bar area, I'm not sure how someone couldn't enjoy this place. As a result of the theming, Florida heat, and people's love of ice cream, the parlor is always very crowded, but worth the wait. While on the pricey side for ice cream, it is very tasty and there is always some type of souvenir bowl or new offering that can't be found anywhere else. Also, how could I forget a personal favorite? The ice cream cookie sandwich is a must-try any time you are in the Magic Kingdom. Don't settle for the one at the ice-cream carts, go get a hand made one at the Ice Cream Parlor! You won't regret it.

The Plaza Restaurant- If the Plaza Ice Cream Parlor was your style atmosphere, but the lines aren't your thing, or you want a real meal, look no further than around the corner. The Plaza Restaurant encompasses the same theming, but with a full menu that is simple and based largely around sandwiches that everyone can enjoy. This location also features ice cream sundae options, but be aware, you do need a reservation for this restaurant a majority of the year. Also, if you aren't okay eating near other people, this may not be the best fit for you. The tables are very close together as a result of the restaurant being very small. That being said, the food is great and it is very easy to get a reservation most of the time.

Casey's Corner- As one of the more iconic Disney counter service meals, this location is a favorite of many guests. The menu has varied slightly from time to time, but has always featured hot dogs and corndogs that are very delicious. Originally, the restaurant featured bleacher style seating, but has recently changed to more space-efficient tables to accommodate more guests. Additionally, the outdoor seating area has been expanded recently and also features many tables. If you time it right, you can even enjoy one of the parades from your outdoor seating area with a virtually unobstructed view. Overall, this location is a personal family favorite and one that virtually every guest will enjoy.

The Crystal Palace- Once again, if you're looking for a sit down restaurant, head over to this wonderful buffet-style restaurant. At this dining location, which is technically the end of the Main Street area, you can have breakfast, lunch, or dinner with Pooh and friends. Now, even though this restaurant is focused towards kids, it is possibly the best buffet on the Disney property and debatably the best dining option in the Magic Kingdom. Although the restaurant is quite large, it is very difficult to get a reservation due to its popularity and the limited table service offerings in the Magic Kingdom. Also worth noting is that Crystal Palace serves breakfast, lunch and dinner, but the the price varies drastically by meal. Breakfast and lunch are somewhat reasonably priced, but dinner is much more expensive. If you're on the dining plan, this is nothing to worry about, but nice to know if you're paying out of pocket for the meal. Be sure to make a reservation as far in advance as you possibly can if you want to eat here. It is one of the most popular restaurants in all of the Disney parks and resorts and is very difficult to acquire last minute.

Main Street Barber Shop and the Main Street Vehicles- Even though these two experiences are not technically attractions, they offer an extra special experience for many guests. First off, is the the barber shop. Many guests ask, "Do they actually cut hair?", and the answer to that is a definite yes. It is actually a full scale barber shop in the Magic Kingdom. Each day, many young kids get their first haircut at Disney and it is always an experience to remember, thanks to the wonderful Disney cast members. The location itself is a little tucked away between the fire station and the front entrances to the Emporium shop, so be careful not to look right past it. Now, in the same general area are the various stops for the main street vehicles. During the day when the crowds are slower on Main Street, Disney offers many unique rideable vehicles that transport guests down the street in style, creating lasting memories for all who get the opportunity to partake.

Main Street, as you can see is something special. You walk into the Magic Kingdom here, round that corner and see the Castle for the very first time. Kids eyes light up, adults fill with joy and ultimately everyone is a kid again. You're enveloped in everything that makes Disney parks special. Here, it's not the attractions, it's not how long the wait times are, it's not how hot it is outside, it's just a feeling that you get and you can't find it anywhere else. Main Street has no "true" attractions, but everyone experiences it to the extent of an attraction which makes it special and hard to believe without experiencing for yourself. Here, Disney accomplishes Walt's original goal to bring families together in a way that cannot be rivaled.

TOMORROWLAND: Tomorrowland is an area often flocked to by guests, but often never truly experienced to its full extent. Originally, the goal of this land was to predict or show the future of tomorrow. Sadly, the Disney company quickly realized, and the hard way I might add, that the future is very hard to predict. Due to that problem, many of the attractions originally found in Tomorrowland no longer exist today, or have been reimagined. Disney was forced to take a different path with the areas design and attractions. The change was subtle, but attempts to predict have all but gone away. What we have today, is a land that appears creative, rather than predictive. Tomorrowland is complete with a newly redesigned Astro Orbiter and Rocket Tower Plaza Station covered with led lights that truly come to life at night. The whole area is uniquely Disney and is very hard to explain in words until we get into the attractions themselves.

Space Mountain- As an iconic Disney World attraction and one of the most famous Disney mountains, it is only natural to want to ride. However, this is definitely not a ride for everyone. If you are a die-hard roller coaster fan, I am sure you can handle Space Mountain and will probably enjoy it. On the flip side, if you have any form of motion sickness, I will caution you to stay off of this attraction. It is designed to be a journey into space and is a rollercoaster in complete darkness. For many, due to its reputation, this sounds like common sense, but from a family member's personal experience nearly 30 years ago, this is not the case. Somehow, they were misinformed that this was a gentle ride through space, and ultimately left Disney with a memory that they didn't particularly intend to have. Even though this was terrible at the time, since they both were very sick afterwards, it is a story that my family will never forget. As an additional warning, the ride has very long wait times a majority of the day, so go early or use a fastpass+ selection if you can. Going back to the attraction itself, it can be very fun for a variety of audiences and anyone capable of trying it should definitely take the time out of their day in the parks to ride Space Mountain.

Tomorrowland Speedway- As an adaptation of the original speedway in Disneyland Anaheim, the Tomorrowland Speedway is an instant classic for the whole family. Despite being a very different track layout than the original, the speedway still offers the fun experience of driving a car for basically all ages. The cars themselves are very small, and virtually impossible to wreck. The speedway is set up to look like there are 4 lanes of cars racing around the track, but each of the cars are on a guide rail. It is an experience for sure, and one that can allow you to watch your children grow over the years from not being able to reach the pedals and having to have an adult do it for them to seeing their eyes light up when they can drive themselves for the very first time. Even if you don't have kids, this is still a wonderful attraction. Even though you're not supposed to, we all know there is nothing better then a makeshift game of bumper cars on rides like this. Also, the cars are actually quite difficult to steer, after the many years of use, so it's always fun to challenge your friends to a race around the track and I guarantee you will have a great time whether you're young or just young at heart.

What many people don't know is that at one time there was a third speedway. After the opening of Disneyland, Walt Disney was approached by many business executives to try to convince him to create for them an attraction. Most of the businesses just wanted the financial gain, so only one sparked his interest enough to follow through. The ride featured small cars very similar to those found at the Tomorrowland Speedway, but unfortunately it is no longer in existence. The speedway was the first and last Disney attraction outside of a Disney theme park.

Cosmic Ray's Starlight Cafe- Directly across from the speedway is this unique counter service offering and a favorite tradition for many guests. Starlight Cafe is a "futuristic" dining location offering three distinct food stations, all sharing one building. Each of the stations features a main item including Chicken, Burgers, or Soups and Salads. Due to the set up, the lines are a bit strange. But, once you understand them it makes the restaurant a little more user friendly. Make sure you're in the line with the item you want listed above the counter and you're good to go! The food is good, but nothing to write home about.

The main draw to Starlight is the size of the restaurant and the availability of both a topping bar and unique entertainment in part of the seating area. As the name suggests, Cosmic Ray is the character that the restaurant is based upon. Cosmic Ray is a piano player (robot) that sings and dances to a variety of songs. Certain parts of the year, he often disappears for a few weeks for special holiday shows and events. A question that often pops up for many guests, who have grown to expect Cosmic Ray is, "Has he gone away?" I can assure you this is not the case, at least not at this time. It is a somewhat little known fact that even though you may not see Ray during these events, the stage actually converts and he is just hidden from the audiences view. The stage is a very clever design and, as with many aspects of Disney World, everything is not always as it appears. When it is time for a special talent group appearance, the stage lowers into the utilidoors (the part of Disney you don't see that is underneath the park) and is then raised back into place. The stage is incredibly advanced for a technology that was developed well before most of the other attractions in today's park.

Auntie Gravity's Galactic Goodies- Despite never actually eating here that I can personally recall, I have never heard a complaint about the offerings at this location. The majority of the menu is ice cream or smoothies and guests seem to really enjoy the products. As far as I know, no news is good news in the realm of Walt Disney World restaurants, because if something's bad you'll always hear about it eventually. One potential problem that I should mention though, is that this location has no seating at all. It is an indoor walk up window connected to a gift shop. So, if you're looking for a place to sit down with your dessert, I'm afraid you're out of luck unless you eat at one of the various tables scattered around the outside of Cosmic Ray's.

Stitch's Great Escape- If you are a returning guest, but it has been a long time since you have been in the parks, you may remember Alien Encounter. Stitch's Great Escape is the more modern, semi kid friendly redesign of that terrifying ride. The attraction set up is very similar to how it was and is basically a large, stationary room with seating in rows around a center platform. When many guests enter the room, they think, "This has to move in some way." I thought the exact same thing. From experience, this is not the case. The shoulder harnesses are just for special effects. Being that it is stationary, nearly any guest can partake in this attraction. A word of caution: it is a somewhat scary ride based on the escape of Stitch in the movie Lilo and Stitch and may not be best for children that are easily frightened. Personally, this is not a must do for me. I don't really care for the attraction and based on the average wait time being near 10-15 minutes during peak times, not many other repeat guests do either. Ultimately, this is a decent ride, but definitely not a must do at the Magic Kingdom. In my opinion, unless you are a huge Stitch fan, your time could probably be better spent somewhere else in the park.

Monster's, Inc. Laugh Floor- One of the more recent, family friendly, additions is the Monster's Inc. Laugh Floor. The attraction is based off of the end of the Monsters Inc. movie (spoiler) where they find that laughter is much more powerful than scream. As a guest, you enter Monstropolis and help Mike Wazowski and friends create energy through laughter for the city. In order to do this, you enter a stage show area and sit in bench-style seats across two sections and begin to interact with the on-screen characters. The characters ask for audience participation and respond based on the situation. No two shows will ever be alike and that gives this attraction infinite repeat value. In regards to the show, it can be for all ages, and everyone can be chosen to interact with the characters no matter what your age. It is a fun show for families and usually has a fairly short wait time. For those summer months, it is also air conditioned and a great place to have some fun while getting out of the heat.

Buzz Lightyear's Space Ranger Spin- Don't let the name fool you, you do not have to spin on this ride and it is a great attraction for families, if not one of the best in the parks. At this time, the ride desperately needs a rehab, but it will always be a favorite for many families. Once you enter the attraction queue you are surrounded by a theme that takes you right into the Toy Story movies. Space Ranger Spin puts you into the roll of a space cadet entering a mission to stop the evil emperor Zurg.

You enter the actual attraction after receiving your orders from Buzz Lightyear and board your vehicle which can hold up to three guests. While on the ride itself you have two laser cannons and a joystick to control the rotation the vehicle allows. Once you begin your mission, you travel through a series of rooms all with Z shaped targets. Your goal is to aim for the Z's and you score points by target location. As a personal tip, aim for the Z on the back of the orange robots arm on the way out of the first room. You will have to turn your vehicle around to see the target. If you hit the dead center of the target you will receive 100,000 points for each bullseye. That being said, at the end of the ride you compare your score to those in your group and each range of scores has a rank based on your performance. Overall, this is a great attraction for a little friendly competition and is always a must-do in the parks.

Walt Disney's Carousel of Progress- As we move on in Tomorrowland, we get to the Carousel of Progress. This is an attraction that many overlook or find boring, but by better understanding the purpose of the attraction and its history, you will enjoy the experience to a much greater extent. The attraction originally debuted at the 1964 World's Fair and was a developing technology that amazed thousands of guests who experienced it for the first time. In the world of audio animatronics, this was the next big thing. The characters in the show moved in a lifelike fashion, despite being robots, and defied what many believed to be impossible. In addition, the current show features a unique technology even today. The theater itself rotates rather than the stage. This allows the stage to remain stable and 3 different scenes to be portrayed without having to create a rotating stage. It was much easier to rotate the guests, rather than the complex audio animatronics. That is why it is referred to as a "carousel" in the title. When experiencing the show, it is a very strange feeling, but adds entertainment value to the attraction that is like nothing anywhere else in the world. The story involved with the production features a family progressing through the generations as technology is developing, showing the past, present, and potential future of technology. By being a gentle journey through the generations, it appeals to nearly any audience, even though some children may not be too interested in the show itself. Now, as you know more of the backstory of the attraction, be sure to take a few minutes to experience this instant classic on your next visit to Walt Disney World.

Tomorrowland Transit Authority PeopleMover- In the center of Tomorrowland stands Rocket Tower Plaza Station, home of the PeopleMover. As an attraction adopted from the original Disneyland park, the PeopleMover holds historical value as well as modern entertainment. The Disneyland park PeopleMover in Anaheim has been abandoned, so as a result, this is the last one left in the world. Originally, the Wedway PeopleMover was designed by Walt Disney and it was set to be a new mainstream form of transportation in Disney's progress city (which later became Epcot). Despite the original plans being scaled back and their potential involvement with the original plans for EPCOT Center, the attraction became a lasting favorite in the Magic Kingdom.

Today, the PeopleMover runs in a constant fashion carrying guests around the top of Tomorrowland. As an attraction that is gentle in pace and easy to walk on without a wait, the PeopleMover is something you can always ride and an experience many guests have deemed their favorite attraction. Once you get to the moving sidewalk that takes you to the ride vehicles themselves, the ride begins. You board the constantly moving attraction via rotating platform. The cars themselves are train like vehicles with forward and rear facing seats. As the experience officially "begins", you are taken through a series of rooms and attractions, viewing them from above. The most unique of these is the journey through Space Mountain. While mostly dark, it is very unique to get to see the attraction at a slower pace or if a young child is too short to ride the ride, they can still be a part of the attraction experience without actually riding it. Your entire journey around Tomorrowland is fairly short, but very enjoyable, especially at night time. You really get to take in all the sites and sounds of the park and even get a great view of the castle from up above the busy streets below.

Astro Orbiter- One of the greatest views in the park is getting to see the Astro Orbiter towering over Tomorrowland. An even better view is experiencing the attraction for yourself, high above Rocket Tower Plaza Station. However, this attraction comes with a subtle warning. If you are afraid of heights or do not do well with spinning, this is probably not a good ride for you. The views are second to none in all of the parks and it really is a very entertaining attraction. The best way to describe the experience is like a simple spinning lift ride, similar to Dumbo, but on a much more "grown up" level. The rockets flying around the tower are on a fairly steep angle and move at a fairly significant speed that is deceiving from the ground. Getting to the attraction is somewhat tough as well and not for those who do not like elevators. The elevators are the only way to the top of the Rocket Tower, and ultimately creates a very slow line. This often leads to wait times well over 30-45 minutes in length. Even with all of these items listed, I cannot recommend the Astro Orbiter enough, especially at night. It is a unique experience that you'll always remember with views you can't find anywhere else.

The Lunching Pad- Directly below the PeopleMover and Astro Orbiter, this counter service dining location offers a small variety of simple food options. With only outdoor seating available, it is not ideal for the summer months, but always a pretty good food option. Personally, I would take the extra few steps over to Cosmic Rays which has similar food and is right around the corner by the Tomorrowland Speedway. Additionally, you have the option of the Tomorrowland Terrace Restaurant near by which has a greater menu variety.

Tomorrowland Terrace Restaurant- Although it is a restaurant that is quick service and has a variety of menu items, the restaurant is only open on a seasonal basis. With that in mind, the Terrace seems to be open more and more as a result of the "off-season" beginning to disappear in the Disney parks. Despite not always being available, it is usually a great seating area and hosts the Magic Kingdom Wishes Dessert Party. The event is an exclusive party for those who wish to eat desserts and have a relaxing place to view the Wishes Fireworks Spectacular.

This option does come at a fairly steep price point and is not a part of the dining plan. Not to cause confusion, the dining area is on the dining plan as a counter service credit, but the dessert party is not on the dining plan at all. Overall the terrace is a great place to eat when it is open and a great, covered area to take a break and enjoy a wonderful view of castle.

With all of the attractions in Tomorrowland covered, you can see why the original concept has been altered over the years. It is still an area of invention and unique opportunities, but ultimately has given up on the extremely difficult goal of predicting tomorrow and moved towards a more realistic goal of creating technologies that will be developed further in the future. Ultimately, as guests, this is about all we can ask for. Nobody can predict the future, but we can create it everyday. That simple goal seems to give every guest an outlook leaving this land that inspires creativity and gives us confidence and hope for success in the future. Walt Disney himself, as a visionary, would truly appreciate what Tomorrowland has become. He always wanted to build the next big thing and he did that every day of his life, defying what many termed impossible through Imagineering marvels.

STORYBOOK CIRCUS: As you move on around the Magic Kingdom, continuing on from Tomorrowland you reach Storybook Circus. Formerly Mickey's Toontown Fair, the area was redesigned as a part of the New Fantasyland expansion. Originally, Toontown was home to a gift shop, a train station, Mickey and Minnie's houses and the Barnstormer rollercoaster. Currently, all of that still exists with the exception of Mickey and Minnie's houses. The rest of the area has just undergone a redesign and theme change. As a result, many names of rides and stores have been changed. Due to the new theme, the Dumbo attraction has been doubled in size and relocated from the center of Fantasyland to Storybook Circus where it matches the new atmosphere.

With all of those changes noted, we'll move on to the new elements. The theming is extensive to say the least. You enter the area and it is obvious the circus has come to town, including an animal themed water area, big top tent shop and even peanuts in the concrete itself to fully immerse the guest in the circus atmosphere. Don't be alarmed if you're worried about allergies like many guests with peanut allergies were. You will not be affected by the peanuts and Disney has made provisions and took this into consideration in the design process. I know this sounds weird, but many guests were worried. Overall, the area is very well done and despite the removal of the two houses, a favorite for many guests, the redesign is extensive and brings a whole new feel to an area that never really had a solid theme in the past.

Dumbo the Flying Elephant- When people think of Disney, their minds go to no other attraction than Dumbo the Flying Elephant. In modern culture, this is one of the main icons of the Disney parks and resorts. Dumbo has been there since the beginning, and is an attraction that many guests hold very close to their heart. As Disney guests, and especially those of us who are repeat guests, we view this ride as a classic. There's nothing too special about it. No frills, no thrills, not even an elaborate theme, but it does accomplish one thing for every guest that you can't find anywhere else.

Dumbo the Flying Elephant has a special way of drawing in families, friends, and all types of guests in a way that no other attraction does. It creates memories and everyone always leaves the Disney parks with a memory from their flight aboard the elephants. Looking at it, you might think it's just another lift and spin ride for kids, but in all honesty it's a lot more than that. It wouldn't be in the Smithsonian if it was just a spinning attraction. It's in the Smithsonian because of what it does for the guest. Trust me, the line is usually pretty manageable, so take the few minutes and create a memory that could last a lifetime. I can't tell you why it happens this way, but it always seems to in some way or another.

The attraction is simple and straightforward as mentioned before. You board your very own Dumbo and fly through the sky. The only difference between this and the original is that there is now two Dumbos that greatly reduce the wait times. Additionally, on the days where the line does get fairly lengthy, the added indoor waiting area, complete with a children's circus themed playground, allows you to wait comfortably with a buzzer like you would at a restaurant. Kids love the attraction, parents love the attraction, and there's just something special about riding Dumbo in the Magic Kingdom.

The Barnstormer- After the remodel, this is one of few things in the area that has not changed too much. The track has remained the same, but the ride theming overall is a little different. To better explain, this is a small rollercoaster with a focus on families and those who don't wish to or cannot ride the other, larger, rollercoasters. With one small drop, the attraction is pretty mild. The only caution I have for guests would be for those that cannot handle a relatively jerky stop or sudden movements. Other than that, the rollercoaster is enjoyable for virtually anyone. It is a very short ride and the wait is usually pretty manageable at near 30 minutes or less on a normal crowd level day.

In regards to the newer theming, the track and the station are exactly the same structurally. A lot of things have been repainted or added to, but the biggest

46

change is the theme change over to a circus style entrance with various props that would be used in a circus act performed by Goofy. The barn that your plane (ride vehicle) "crashes" through is no longer a barn, but rather a large billboard sign that does virtually the same thing. The Barnstormer is a lot of fun, but be aware, at just over 6 foot tall, the ride vehicles are a bit tight for me to fit in and they usually seat two people per row. It can make for a cramped ride for two full size adults, but is still incredibly enjoyable. When you're tall, part of the fun is just trying to get out of the plane!

The Storybook Circus Railroad Station- As a part of the same railroad that leaves from the Main Street Station and circles the park, the Storybook Circus Station is the only station that has been recently redesigned from ground up. Questionably, this station is one of the more beautifully and elaborately decorated parts of Magic Kingdom. The station itself is very classy and almost feels upscale in a way. From the elaborate brickwork out front to the accompanying detail in the bathrooms adjoined, the area really is quite beautiful. I know that's a lot to say about a train station and some bathrooms, but it really is something special and is a level of detail that you will only find at Walt Disney World. A lot of times the details are what really sets Disney parks apart from all other theme parks. No other company is going to put that much time and effort into a bathroom and a place to board a train, which is what makes this simple area special to many guests.

Pete's Silly Side Show- Another unique part of Storybook Circus is the opportunity to meet your favorite Disney characters in their circus, or rather, performance attire. Four of everyones favorite characters: Minnie, Goofy, Donald and Daisy are all present with special backdrops that offer a very unique photo opportunity. These costumes worn by the characters, are only ever found at this location. It is a neat experience that everyone should see at least once and, lets be honest, we all want our picture taken with the characters.

With all this being said, that covers the attractions in this area. I know many die hard Disney fans don't like the changes in this area, and the move away from the Toontown theming into the circus theming, but it's really just nostalgia when you get down to it. There always has to be new experiences, and if there wasn't, why would we keep coming back time after time? Like Walt Disney said, the parks will never be finished, the world is changing and the parks will have to grow and adapt in essence as they have been doing for many years. Things have to change, no matter how hard that change is to make. The parks aren't what they use to be, but that's not always a bad thing. They grow and continue to develop, and that brings us to the largest expansion in Magic Kingdom history: New Fantasyland.

FANTASYLAND: Originally, Fantasyland was a part of the park that was fairly small in area, but was the most densely populated with attractions. You could, and still can, get off one attraction and get right back on to another a few steps away. After the expansion, the area changed, and in my opinion, it changed for the better. Originally the theming was minimal. A few buildings fit the fantasy concept, but most of the attractions had the same bland entrance with a different sign and a different color pattern. When the expansion and redesign began, it began with the remodel of The Many Adventures of Winnie the Pooh.

Originally, The Many Adventures of Winnie the Pooh was just as simple as the other attractions in its exterior design. After it was redesigned, a new idea was put into place in a variety of different ways throughout Fantasyland. Pooh was the first step. At the attraction, the line queue was redesigned to be more kid-friendly, more hands on, and ultimately more immersive for the guests. You could have fun while you waited with little games and activities and that concept moved on into other aspects of the expansion. Now, the entire land is incredibly immersive and New Fantasyland takes that immersion factor to a whole new level.

You really get to become a part of the stories, from being a guest in the Beast's mansion to entering the Seven Dwarfs mine. The area doesn't just show you the movies like it once did, it truly puts you in the movies. With that being said, this expansion and redesign of a majority of Fantasyland comes as a change, which many avid Disney guests are always hesitant of. Still, it's hard to see how it couldn't have been a change for the better. Today, we have a Fantasyland that meets and exceeds the expectations of the guests in a way that it never fully captured in the past. Now, as you can imagine, a lot has changed so we'll take a look at every attraction just as we have with every other land so far.

"it's a small world"- Small World is an attraction that has changed many times, but has ultimately stood the test of time. No matter how simple this gentle boat ride is, it always puts a smile on your face. It has truly become a Disney icon. In a similar way to Dumbo, "it's a small world" is what every guest to the Magic Kingdom has heard about for years and the nostalgia factor draws in thousands of guests everyday. It's something that everyone in the family can enjoy and appreciate. Ultimately, it's one of those things in life that really makes you appreciate the small things. It puts a smile on your face and thats all it really needs to do. It is a no frills ride through various groups of children singing "it's a small world" in their native language. Somehow, it is always enjoyable and something that every guest should take a few minutes to enjoy, especially since the wait time is usually quite short. The attraction itself was another adaption from Disneyland that stuck here at Walt Disney World. Although very different from the Disneyland version, this attraction, which originally debuted at the 1964 World's Fair, has become a Disney icon that has to be a part of any Disney vacation.

Peter Pan's Flight- As possibly one of the most unique "dark rides" in the history of Walt Disney World, Peter Pan's Flight carries guest of all ages through the "sky" over various scenes replicating those found in the Peter Pan film. The family friendly experience is very unique to Disney. You get in your own personal pirate ship, which holds up to three people, and take off with the help of Tinker Bell's pixy dust. Without experiencing it for yourself, the sensation is a little strange to explain. It feels as if you are on a hanging rollercoaster, but the pirates ship sways ever so gently giving it a floating effect that only Disney could create. The standby queue for the attraction is just as clever. Recently the queue line was transformed into the home that is found in the movie and gives each guest an experience in line, as is the growing trend at Walt Disney World. It is a trend that I believe will soon cover all of the attractions across the parks. Moving back to the attraction itself, it is definitely worth the wait, but be aware that the wait time can often be well over an hour for a fairly short ride. Peter Pan's Flight is definitely a good use of a fastpass+. Additionally, if you can't get the fastpass+ or do not wish to use it as one of your three for the day, get there early or try and ride it very late at night to avoid a majority of the crowds. No matter what it takes, this is probably one of the highest rated attractions on my personal must do "list" and one that every guest should enjoy.

Mickey's PhilharMagic- PhilharMagic is one of the most original, but also one of the most outdated attractions in the parks. To explain what I mean, the ride is basically a 4D show that incorporates a 3D film with smells and effects that fill the theatre. The film on its own is a compilation of various Disney movies that have been worked into the shows goal, which is to find Mickey's Sorcerer hat. Before I give too much away, I'll get back to my point. In this day and age 3D has become pretty commonplace and is even found in many people's houses. So, when guests go to the show, a lot of them come out disappointed in the 3D quality. When it was first opened, I experienced it and thought "Wow, that was incredible!", but today it lacks that wow factor due to the great advancements in 3D technology. Now, don't let that keep you away from the show. It is still a lot of fun and a unique attraction, but go into it with managed expectations. The screen itself is incredibly large and grows with the show. That in itself is pretty neat and the extra effects really transform the experience and make it worth going to see. Ultimately, everyone can enjoy PhilharMagic and the wait time is never very long, so it's worth checking out at least once.

Prince Charming Regal Carrousel- The carrousel is a ride that doesn't change much no matter where you are. Some are larger than others, but ultimately, they all do the same thing. However, the carousel at both Walt Disney World and Disneyland have a special backstory that makes them a little more interesting. Even though this story is not advertised or posted with the attraction, it is assumed to be true. As I have mentioned previously, a somewhat bad experience Walt Disney and his daughter had at a carousel ultimately inspired Disneyland. So, Walt felt it fit to have a carousel in the park and one that exceeded expectations. Each of the parks have a special carousel, but the story of the one in Disney World is pretty unique. Prince Charming Regal Carrousel was brought in from another location and had been hand picked for the Magic Kingdom. Once it was purchased, the ride was stripped down and repainted. In that process, no two horses were made alike and that still remains true today. To maintain the attraction, these horses have to be taken down and repainted by hand in sequence so that the horses all get replaced over time. Extra horses are always on hand to fill in for one being painted.

While those are the facts behind the attraction, there is a rumor amongst Disney fans that claim that there are two horses that are particularly special. One for Prince Charming and one for Cinderella, each with their own identifying pattern. For example, Cinderella's supposedly has a bow on it's tail. In a similar regard, while on the carrousel take a minute to notice how shiny everything is nearly all the time. The poles that the horses are attached to are polished almost constantly to maintain that special shine and, as mentioned, the horses are painted on a cycle so they never look outdated. In the end, take a few minutes to enjoy this special attraction and to realize the details that separate it from every other carousel. It's truly hard to believe that you can still take a ride on a carousel that works flawlessly nearly one hundred years after it was originally built in 1917!

Pinocchio Village Haus- Once you get done with a ride on the carousel, take a few steps over to the Village Haus. This area, the only Pinocchio themed part of any park, is one of the best counter service options in the Magic Kingdom. The menu consists of flatbread pizzas, chicken, salads, and even garlic bread knots. It's not a standard theme park dining experience by a long shot. The interior is very intricate, featuring a design that looks very much like Geppetto's house in the film. Additionally, the interior has a few unique features that make it distinctly Disney. For example, in one room of seating there is a large glass window that allows you to see right into "it's a small world". As simple as that sounds, it's quite a bit of fun to wave at the boats below and have a little entertainment during your lunch or dinner.

Something else often overlooked about the Village Haus is that if you are looking for a unique view of the fireworks you can take a seat in the outdoor seating area and enjoy, in my opinion, one of the best views of the Wishes Nighttime Spectacular. As a part of the show, some fireworks are launched off of the building roofs near by, as well as behind you, and it makes for a truly immersive fireworks experience. That being said, it is also extremely loud inside and outside of Pinocchio's during the fireworks. For some smaller children it can become a very frightening place to eat during the show. If you aren't phased by loud noises and want a whole new fireworks experience, be sure to check out this restaurant. You may have to get your seat about an hour in advance, but by the time you eat, it will be just about time for the show to get started.

The Friar's Nook- This dining location is another counter service option in the area. After the location underwent a menu change near the opening of New Fantasyland, many Disney enthusiasts became avid fans of their new offerings. The menu is a little out of the ordinary offering various macaroni dishes that feature unique toppings, including a pot roast macaroni and cheese, which is pretty hard to forget. As weird as it sounds, it is one of the most loved new items in all of the parks by the guests. The location itself is just a simple walk up, outdoor, counter service location. The seating is very limited and is exclusively outdoors. Even though there is no "designated" seating area, you can always walk over to the Village Haus to eat indoors or there are many benches in the general area. With all of this being said, take a minute to try the pot roast macaroni, because you can't get it anywhere else and it's a great meal that keeps you full for a pretty long time. Also, since you only need to buy one or two items for a full meal, it is actually a pretty budget-friendly option as well.

Storybook Treats- Almost directly next to The Friar's Nook is the second location in the Magic Kingdom to get ice cream. Different from the ice cream found at the parlor on Main Street, this location focuses on soft serve based ice cream. Everything they sell is ice cream based and they only sell dessert items. The desserts are good, but not too special. I would suggest making the walk over to Main Street for a better selection, but that's just my opinion. I prefer hand dipped ice cream opposed to soft serve, but its great to have options so you can choose which you prefer. Just as with The Friar's Nook, the seating here is very limited, but there is the alternate seating previously mentioned as well.

The Many Adventures of Winnie the Pooh- As an attraction that replaced a favorite for many, The Many Adventures of Winnie the Pooh often gets mixed reviews from Disney enthusiasts. Originally, the attraction was Mr. Toad's Wild Ride, which is still found in Disneyland today. Many people loved that attraction and it's closure was never fully explained in a way that appeased the enthusiasts. The mixed feelings about the attraction cause a lot of biased opinions of The Many Adventures of Winnie the Pooh. Personally, I don't remember ever riding Mr. Toad's Wild Ride, so I can give you a fairly unbiased opinion. As a simple dark ride, the attraction creates a fun experience for the whole family that is gentle and tells a story. After the remodel occurred the attraction's queue became much more immersive and seemed to cut down wait times significantly. Additionally, the wait became much more enjoyable for smaller kids, giving them something to do while passing the time in line. Ultimately, if you have kids or just want a fun, simple, enjoyable, attraction be sure to ride The Many Adventures of Winnie the Pooh despite what many of the Mr. Toad fans might say about the attraction.

Cheshire Café- As a counter service location that used to get very little business, I was surprised at the line I witnessed last time I was in the parks. Little did I know, they had added a special menu item that I had to try. As the only place on property to get the item, the line can get a little long. But, the fact that they only sell coffee and a few other specialty items keeps the wait from being too big of a factor. The new offering is basically a cup full of cake and icing. As simple as that sounds, it is quite tasty and a very good dessert item that is often overlooked. What sets it apart is creativity. The dessert is layered in the cup with icing between each layer and makes for that perfect piece of cake with every bite. Disney has even gone to the extent of changing the flavor offerings by season and for special events. As fun as this dessert is, the café has a fairly limited menu, but it's always worth looking into.

Mad Tea Party- As Disney's take on a "scrambler" spinning ride, this is not an attraction for someone who doesn't really enjoy spinning. I have experienced the attraction first hand and will not do that again anytime soon. On the ride itself, the floor of the attraction spins along with the tea cup that you ride in. You control the spin rate of the cup, but not of the floor. That concept is very misleading for many people and ultimately how someone got me on the tea cups in the first place. Many believe that as long as you don't spin the cup, it will not spin. This seems like common sense, but it is not true because the floor rotates in a series of smaller circles that causes every guest to spin. Be sure to take that into consideration before someone talks you into the ride as well.

The attraction does really excel for those who love a good spinning attraction. If you choose, you can spin at an incredible speed and each teacup holds quite a few guests. Additionally, the Alice in Wonderland theming is quite unique. Where else can you ride in a larger then life teacup that spins? Lastly, for those of you who have been to Disneyland, this version of the ride is actually covered and not exposed to the elements. As a result, it operates rain or shine contrary to the one in California. Also, if you time it right, you can even ride the teacups with Alice and the Mad Hatter themselves! That will make for an experience that will definitely be hard to forget!

Seven Dwarfs Mine Train- Now that we've made it through the original Fantasyland attractions, we can move on to the latest and greatest addition to the Disney parks, New Fantasyland. New Fantasyland is next level Disney and the Seven Dwarfs Mine Train is a great example of this new era of innovation. If you even get near the attraction you can tell it is something special. The level of theming and the elaborate setting created for the attraction and the technology involved with the system is hard to rival with any other Disney experience. The Mine Train really encompasses everything that creates the Disney difference. It is elaborate, creative, and detailed, but above all, functional. Just by walking past the attraction, you can tell that the ride vehicles have a completely different sound. They are undoubtedly the quietest rollercoaster vehicles I have ever witnessed and it is a pleasant surprise both on and off of the attraction.

No other ride in the world comes close in the family friendly roller coaster category. As a unique combination of dark ride and thrill ride, the Mine Train is something that everyone can enjoy. The attraction itself is the smoothest roller coaster I have ever been on. Part of that is due to the fact that the ride vehicle sways, removing any jerkiness that a lot of rollercoasters create. Additionally, it adds to the experience itself. It is a legit mine car that you would picture in your head. This simple roller coaster also has a short section of animatronics part way through the ride that really brings home the feeling of being with the Seven Dwarfs in the mine.

All of these details should be taken into consideration when choosing to ride the Seven Dwarfs Mine Train, but if you are very motion sensitive I would sit this one out. Personally, it does not bother me to ride this attraction, but many others do. I have never been able to comfortably ride Expedition Everest or Rock 'n' Roller Coaster, for example. So, from personal experience, it isn't much of a factor in creating motion sickness and nearly anybody can usually do just fine on the Mine Train. The attraction almost always has a ridiculously long line, but it is one of the few attractions I would say is worth the wait. I always try to get a fastpass+ if I can, but they are very scarce most of the year. The Seven Dwarfs Mine Train is a great way to start or end a day at the Magic Kingdom and really brings your friends or family together for a unique experience that everyone can enjoy.

Enchanted Tales with Belle- If you have been to the Disney parks before, this attraction may seem familiar. A similar experience used to be in the parks, but this new version took the old idea to a whole new level. As more of a show than a ride, anyone can experience Enchanted Tales with Belle. It is an experience that is focused on small children, but is actually pretty cool for all ages to do at least once. When you enter the attraction, you enter a cottage just like the one her father lives in throughout the movie Beauty and the Beast. Once it is your turn to start, you and your group enter Belle's father's workshop and you are surrounded by neat inventions as your tour begins. As that room finishes up, something very unique happens (spoiler, the mirror is not a mirror). After that, you interact with one of Belle's friends from the castle and then move on to the actual short show itself that everyone can get involved with. Once the "stage" is set, Belle joins you in person to tell a story. At the end of the experience, the kids are always amazed and the adults realize they have witnessed something incredibly inventive and one of a kind. That being said, most adults that partake in the attraction usually don't have a desire to do it again. It's one of those been there done that attractions for adults, but kids will want to do it over and over again.

Be Our Guest Restaurant- Continuing on in the Beauty and the Beast theme, we get to my personal favorite themed restaurant on property, Be Our Guest. From the moment you arrive at the bridge leading over to the restaurant, you know it's going to be something special. For most, Cinderella's Royal Table is the prime spot to take any princess lover. In my opinion, Be Our Guest is far better than Cinderella's Royal Table in the way of both food and character experience. When you enter Be Our Guest, it feels like you're stepping right into the movie. The restaurant itself was designed to look just like the movie rather than just having characters placed in a restaurant like many other character meals do.

Once you get across the bridge, you enter the Beast's castle and it is just how you could imagine it in your most elaborate dreams. It exceeds expectations in ways that are hard to explain. First, you have a row of knights armor that lines the hall. Then, you have three themed seating areas based on the the West Wing, the Ball Room, and the Library. Each of these rooms are very elaborate, but fit the design created for the movie to perfection. In the west wing, the rose from the film has been recreated in hologram form and the petals fall off the stem slowly as time progresses. The library features a large sculpture of Bell and Beast that doubles as an elaborate music box. Lastly, the main and largest seating area of the restaurant is the ball room. Surprisingly, it is nearly identical to the one in the movie and can really take your breath away. The floors are polished like mirrors and the facade window is even complete with simulated snow to really complete the full immersion factor that is found throughout the entire restaurant.

In regards to the actual dining times and menu options, it gets pretty complicated. First off, currently they have been testing a breakfast menu for a quick service dining option. Once lunch time rolls around a new menu starts, but the counter service dining type remains the same. Counter service at Be Our Guest is quite different than most counter service locations. When you enter the building at lunch, you use a kiosk system to order your food then you just go find a table and they bring your food to your location. The RFID chip in your magic band gives the cast members your exact location in the restaurant so they just bring your food out to your location. The lunch menu options are very good and the desserts are even better. The best part of the counter service options is that you get to enjoy the exact same setting as you would at dinner for about half the price.

If you want that high end dining experience with a full, extensive, menu of high-end food, be sure to look into the table service dinner option. During the dinner hours, most of the food has a slight french influence that is not off-putting to most, but is noticeable enough to be unique. However, that higher quality comes with a higher price as well as a higher demand for reservations. Currently, Be Our Guest is one of the top three most difficult restaurants to get reservations for. Even though I know that was a lot of information all about one restaurant, don't let it overwhelm you. No matter what dining experience you choose to have at Be Our Guest, it will undoubtedly be a highlight of your trip to the Magic Kingdom.

Gaston's Tavern- As with a lot of dining options at the Disney Parks, if you don't like the offerings at one restaurant, walk a few steps and you'll find something different at the next one. Gaston's Tavern is a perfect example of this. If you don't want to take the time or effort to go to Be Our Guest, be sure to check out Gaston's for a creative, but extremely quick dining experience. With a limited, but unique menu, Gaston's is a highly themed area that even carries over into the food items. Food offerings consist of just a few items including the signature dish, pork shank. As weird as that sounds for a theme park food offering, it is actually very good. If that isn't strange enough on its own, you can pair it with a Disney exclusive drink called LeFou's Brew. Despite what the name implies, this is a non-alcoholic drink that tastes similar to what you can imagine a frozen, very sweet, apple juice would taste like. Topping the drink and giving it its name is a Mango flavored froth that has a very unique texture. The frozen part of the drink is an adaptation of what is sold at California Adventure in the new Cars Land if you have ever had the opportunity to experience that incredible place. The actual taste is pretty good, but it's more of a dessert rather than a drink. Overall, the food is pretty good, but not everyone will be interested in what they have to offer.

Under The Sea-Journey of The Little Mermaid- Moving away from the dining locations of Fantasyland, we get to the newest dark ride addition to the Disney parks and resorts. As soon as you enter the attraction queue, you start to witness the next level theming that is found throughout New Fantasyland. From the greeting from Scuttle the seagull, to the crab hide and go seek game throughout the line, you can tell that Disney Imagineering made great strides to create a fun and original attraction. After leaving the queue, you board a clam shell and take a journey under the sea. As a family ride that accommodates any guest, it's hard not to leave the Journey of The Little Mermaid without a smile on your face. As with the queue, the attraction itself features unique Imagineering firsts. All of the animatronics have incredibly life like movements and are incredibly fluid. You can really tell that the intent was for the animatronics to be life like, but also have a distinctly animated appearance, just as they do in the classic movie we all know and love. Upon exiting the ride, make sure to stop by next door at Ariel's Grotto for a chance to meet Ariel in person and even see some of her latest and greatest under the sea finds.

Cinderella's Royal Table- With one last dining option in Fantasyland, I left the constant guest favorite for last. Cinderella's Royal Table is an icon of the Disney Parks. For those of you who don't know, this dining location is the only way to go up into the castle itself. You can almost always walk through the castle, but only the restaurant gives you the true, royal, dining experience. Now personally, I have not had the opportunity to eat in the castle in many years. Over the years, the menu has changed very little, but has always been more about the experience rather than the food. There is something about the location that keeps people coming back no matter what the food is like. The menu items are upscale for both lunch and dinner, but there is a simpler breakfast menu. Additionally, for all the kids and adults alike, Cinderella and friends come right over to your table and interact with you and your family.

With all of that being said, I believe that the draw to the restaurant is not the food or even the character experience, but rather the incredibly beautiful scenery within the restaurant. The dining area is incredible, complete with floor to ceiling stained glass, unique lighting fixtures, and a view of Fantasyland that you can't find anywhere else. As beautiful as this location is, it is worth noting that the price is very high, and you are paying more for the experience than the food itself. Due to the price, in order to eat here on the standard Disney Dining Plan you must use two table service dining credits for each individuals' meal. So, if you choose to eat here, you may have to cut out a meal somewhere else to accommodate the extra credit required or pay out of pocket. If this is still on your must-do list for the Magic Kingdom, be sure to make reservations 180 days in advance due to the fact that reservations are EXTREMELY hard to obtain.

LIBERTY SQUARE: Just down the hill from Fantasyland lies possibly one of the most overlooked parts of the Magic Kingdom. At the end of that short journey down the hill, you walk right into the time frame of the founding of America. Liberty Square is unique and original, but also quite small in scale. Most people ride the few attractions that are there and never take the time to look around and spend a little extra time exploring the area. During the day, I can't say that I blame them. Liberty Square can get very crowded in the afternoons. Thankfully, it gets much more exciting at night, especially on those rare nights where the park isn't too terribly crowded and you can just walk around and enjoy everything Liberty Square has to offer. The Haunted Mansion really comes alive at night (no pun intended) and the views from the riverboat near dawn are hard to pass up. As you can see, the square is much more entertaining than it appears to be and hopefully the following descriptions convince you to take your time and enjoy it all you can while you're in the parks.

The Haunted Mansion- As the main draw to the area, The Haunted Mansion is a classic attraction that has developed over the years into an Imagineering marvel. Originally, The Haunted Mansion was very forward thinking, and encompassed a variety of new and old design techniques. As you begin the pre-show of sorts for the attraction, you enter a room with no windows and no doors and the rest you'll have to experience for yourself. After that, you board your vehicle, or "doom buggy" as they call it, and take a tour through the mansion filled with ghosts trapped for all eternity. As you can imagine, this isn't really an attraction for small children. A lot of kids enjoy the ride, but if your child is scared somewhat easily, I would probably pass on this experience. It is not scary to the level of most haunted houses, but could definitely be frightening for some audiences.

Moving on to the ride features themselves, Imagineering is at its best in an attraction like this. If you're one of those people that just wants to be amazed by the "magic" of Disney, you may want to skip these paragraphs, but the details are actually pretty incredible. Two of the original spectacles of this ride were the ball room and the hitchhiking ghosts. The ball room is basically a room of ghosts at a party that appears to the viewer as if they are real-life hologram-style ghosts. In reality, this a clever illusion, because this level of hologram is basically impossible, even with modern technology. The illusion is created using a gigantic piece of glass that is placed across the balcony that you view the "ghosts" through from above. The gigantic piece of glass is very hard to see in the poorly lit conditions and without flaw in the material, the illusion is extremely successful. The secret to the illusion is that the glass basically reflects a series of animatronics that are out of view of the guest creating the appearance of ghost-like images in the ball room.

The second illusion of the attraction, the hitchhiking ghosts, creates an image in a mirror that a ghost is in your doom buggy. Just as above, this is a seemingly complex illusion that is actually quite simple. It uses basically the same principle of the ball room, just modified to achieve a different goal. Unfortunately, the hitchhiking ghost illusion has been replaced with a more modern, electronic, system that creates a more convincing illusion. Once you know these details, you can usually see the glass or understand how it works, but you are always amazed at just how well it creates convincing illusions that mesmerize guests each and every day.

Liberty Square Riverboat- The riverboat isn't always the most interesting attraction, but it is a great break from the hectic nature of the parks and lets you relax and enjoy the views from around the park. The scenery is really the best part of the attraction. Once you board this multi-story steam powered paddlewheel, it makes a fairly long journey around Tom Sawyer Island, offering great photo opportunities for both Liberty Square and almost the entirety of Frontierland. Some guests will like this much more then others, but I would say anyone can enjoy the attraction. However, not everyone will. What I mean by that is simple. The people who are non stop, commando style, Disney goers won't want to take the time to ride a boat in a circle. It just won't be their style or purpose in going to the Magic Kingdom. Contrary, someone who is in the parks just to have a good time and relax will most likely really enjoy the riverboat. As you can see, it all depends on the experience you desire to have.

Even if the Riverboat doesn't sound like something you'd like, if you, the kids, or any guest for that matter get exhausted in the parks, this is a great place to take a break and get out of the sun for a few minutes. One thing to be aware of though is that the riverboat often runs on a strange schedule, so it is not always open. But, when it is, the wait is usually pretty non-existent. On a sort of random side note, be sure to look at the water the riverboat floats in. For years the discolored water seemed out of the ordinary in the Disney parks, but recently I found out that the water is actually intentionally dyed in order to cover the track that guides the riverboat. I always thought it was weird that the water here was so murky when all the other water on Disney property seemed fairly clear. It just goes to show you that Disney really has thought of just about everything to keep the magic alive!

Colombia Harbour House- Directly between The Haunted Mansion and The Hall of Presidents is this early-american counter service offering. For one of the most overlooked Magic Kingdom dining experiences, this restaurant has become a sort of hidden gem. The location really makes the destination. The food is pretty good, but often a little weird to eat since it is a mostly fish based menu. It doesn't always smell too appealing in the Florida heat. That being said, if you're looking for a pretty good meal and an even better dining area, be sure to look into the Harbour House.

With all of that being said about the restaurant, I feel like I should tell you a little more since there really isn't much to say about the menu. Some Disney parks enthusiasts might not appreciate me sharing this, because it's a bit of hidden gem of Magic Kingdom, but there is something special about this restaurant a lot of guests overlook. When walking down the hill to Liberty Square, take a look at the windows above you. That archway is actually a seating area for the restaurant when the upstairs dining room is open. Now, I know that sounds simple, but it is really an incredible place to sit and get away from the crowds to just take a few minutes to enjoy the views out the window at one of the most beautiful sections of the Magic Kingdom. You can sit here for hours if you have the time, but be sure to check it out, because you never know, this simple area could really be one of the highlights of your trip as it is for all the guests who probably won't like me including it in this guide!

Liberty Square Market- Although this isn't really a restaurant or an attraction, I'll take a minute and throw it in here for a simple reason. Lots of times when my family is at Walt Disney World, after eating fried food and all kinds of not so great things, it is nice to have something fresh. This is the place to get something fresh and simple. They have fresh fruit in a sort of market atmosphere for a majority of the day and it really is a nice break from the "fast food" and a great use of a snack option on the Disney Dining Plan.

The Hall of Presidents- For many, this attraction is nothing more than a good air conditioned place to take a nap, but for anyone who really appreciates history or politics, this is a can't-miss attraction. In the waiting area, there is a variety of unique, presidential, and early american artifacts that really bring the history into the attraction itself. Once you enter the theatre, you take your seat in one of over one hundred seats and prepare for the show. As it begins, it goes through a brief history of America's independence then moves on to the main section of the show. The screen opens slowly and one of the best animatronics in

Disney history, Abraham Lincoln, stands and recites the Gettysburg address. As clever as that is, the back story is what makes the Abraham Lincoln animatronic so unbelieved. In preparation for the 1964 World's Fair, Walt Disney's high level group of engineers prepared the most life-like animatronic ever produced. This robot essentially changed the realm of possibilities and ultimately developed into all of the animatronics you can experience in the Disney parks today.

The invention took the world by storm. Through a series of hydraulic, liquid based pressure changes, Abraham Lincoln could become animated and interact in the most lifelike way imaginable. Amazingly, the technology had very few complications. At first there was a funny issue that occurred when a hose decided to give out. When this happened, red fluid that was used in the hydraulic system spilled out and made the animatronic appear as if it was bleeding. As you can imagine, this looked less than magical to say the least. Once that issue was fixed, the technology developed into what is found in many Disney attractions today. Despite the early setbacks, the modern animatronics are just as stunning as they must have been in 64'.

Moving back to the experience itself, once Abraham Lincoln finishes, the rest of the presidents appear on stage and each say their name. It is a very simple show, but definitely a sort of hidden Disney classic once you can appreciate the backstory. As you can imagine, it isn't all that interesting for a majority of kids and even most adults, but always offers a great break that can even be educational. When the backstory becomes known, the attraction takes on a different meaning for the guest. When you can appreciate the story, it becomes an experience that makes you really understand the thought and passion that every Disney Imagineer has put into their work over the years and even today.

Sleepy Hollow- As an additional dessert-based restaurant in the Magic Kingdom that is just as good as all the others, a few food items make Sleepy Hollow really stand out. One of those is possibly the best quick service breakfast item on property, the waffle sandwiches. As weird as this item sounds, they are incredible. The waffles feature everything from a hazelnut type spread to even more elaborate combinations. Additionally, this location is the only place in the Magic Kingdom that serves funnel cakes. Who doesn't love a funnel cake? To top it all off, you can even get ice-cream and, in the winter months, hot chocolate.

Liberty Tree Tavern- As one of the last table service meals left to mention in the Magic Kingdom, this is one that you can actually get a reservation at fairly late in the reservation window. I've never quite understood why this is; the food is really good and the experience is just as good, if not better. The menu has undergone quite a few changes over the years, but has never been a bad meal choice. The lunch offerings are all based off of a menu that takes it's influence from early American staples that you would possibly find on a Thanksgiving table. Dinner really brings this Thanksgiving style of eating into full scale with a family style meal that features everything from turkey to mashed potatoes. There's something here for everyone, and it really gives you that homemade meal that everyone wishes they could eat every day.

The Diamond Horseshoe- To be completely honest, I'm really hesitant to even include this in the guide because it's hardly ever open. The Diamond Horseshoe has always been open seasonally, but more recently it seems to be open a little more often due to increased crowds and record attendance numbers in the parks. When The Diamond Horseshoe is actually open, the menu is pretty simple and based on sandwiches and salads. In Disneyland, I understand this is one of the more popular dining locations (called the Golden Horseshoe at Disneyland), but unfortunately that is far from the case in Walt Disney World. Just be sure to manage your expectations if you are used to going to the one at Disneyland when you visit The Diamond Horseshoe at the Magic Kingdom. On the bright side, it is believed that the restaurant will be open for lunch and dinner as a table service option in the near future.

As you can see, there are a lot of experiences that get overlooked in Liberty Square and a few aren't even in the attractions themselves. Always keep your eyes open when you're there, because the details really make the experience. For a quick example, look at the center piece of the area itself. The "Liberty Bell", or rather a replica of the Liberty Bell, sits right in the middle of the square. Very few people know, the bell itself is an exact replica of the original. When guests first hear this, they always say it can't be possible because it appears so small, but in reality it is the exact same as the original (minus the crack).

It is really unique to see that level of detail in the parks and what truly sets Disney apart from all other theme parks. Everything is special no matter if it is as elaborate as bringing "ghosts" to life in The Haunted Mansion, or just the little details of the decor. There is something about the area that makes it special when you realize it's history and the backstory involved. For me, the real draw to the area is at night. You can sit, relax, watch a parade and even just enjoy the view. It really is something unique that is incredibly hard to explain. I'm not quite sure if it's the twinkling lanterns or the quiet nature of the area, but it creates a feeling that you can't find anywhere else and that really makes you realize everything that makes the Magic Kingdom so special.

FRONTIERLAND: As mentioned above about the Liberty Square area, Frontierland also has a unique, distinctly "magical" feel to it at night. What sets it apart from the square is that it focuses on the frontier rather than the early history of America. Even though these are distinctly different themes, they really come together in a simple way. As for Frontierland itself, it is usually a favorite for guests due to the fact that it includes two of Disney's most iconic mountains.

Despite the mountains, the area really has quite a bit more to offer that a lot of people overlook. For example, there is always Tom Sawyer Island, which many of the most frequent guests have never stepped foot on. A lot of people don't give the simpler, timeless attractions a chance and they are doing themselves a great disservice by doing so. In some ways it is understandable, but as I've said before, you can never see and do everything. However, you can always enjoy the little things and should always take the time to enjoy what sets Disney apart. It shouldn't be about the attractions, but rather the whole experience.

For a lot of guests, the memories aren't from the attractions, but by experiencing the little moments that bring a family together. When talking about Frontierland, one of those personal experiences comes to mind. Surprisingly, it was on Splash Mountain of all attractions. I was much younger and traveling with friends, as well as family. We were heading down the final hill on Splash Mountain, and our friends' hat flew off. We weren't too worried about it, but we get to the bottom of the hill and the guy behind us reaches forward and says, "Hey, your hat came off." and hands it back to him. It was something we never expected. The guy behind us was nice enough and fast enough to catch the hat and we laughed about it for the rest of the day. Somehow, I'll never forget that experience.

I can't tell you if we got off that ride soaked or completely dry, but what I can tell you is that we all had a huge smile on our face. Those are the experiences that I remember from Frontierland and the simple things that I will always remember. Really, that's the main reason for writing this book. Never lose sight of why you are going to the parks in the first place. Most of the time, it's not for the attractions, but rather for the people you get to spend the time with. Frontierland really lends itself to some of these great moments that will last a lifetime. Special experiences like this seem to happen at Disney all the time, and it's one of the many, many aspects of the vacation that really makes you go home with a smile on your face.

Splash Mountain- After telling that story, we'll jump right into Splash Mountain. A lot of people are afraid to get on this ride. For one reason, it seems like the drop is ridiculously large from the outside and it is a pretty long drop. But, the other reason is that they don't want to get wet. In regards to the first excuse, I'll tell you that it's over quick, but if you think your stomach can handle it, the rest of the attraction is well worth the few seconds of fear the drop creates. Another good point is that a lot of people really love the drop, so you never know, you may just find something new to love in the Disney Parks by facing a fear.

The other issue is a little more difficult to pin point an answer for. Some days, you will get off Splash Mountain virtually dry, but other days you leave without a dry spot on you. It's kind of a "luck of the draw" scenario that you can make a good guess at before getting on. When you pass in front of the mountain on the way to the entrance, check and see if the water canon that fires out the front, over the boats, is on. If it is, you have about a one in five chance of getting off drenched. If it's not, you're in luck and will usually get off fairly dry.

One more point is worth mentioning though. Try to ignore all these reasons you would not get on the attraction. Take my word for it, if you get on, you're almost guaranteed to have fun. The interior of the ride takes you through the Uncle Remus tale of Br'er Rabbit. The story is unique, clever, and leaves you smiling the entire ride. As I've mentioned above, you never know what kind of special experience you will have on Splash Mountain. It is an unpredictable experience and creates a huge draw for guests. Sometimes, you can catch the line short early in the morning or late at night, but be aware, it is a thrill ride as you will be able to see from the outside.

Country Bear Jamboree- The Country Bear Jamboree is another Disney classic. Personally, it's not a favorite of mine, but a lot of guests have made it a must-do no matter how simple and corny the entire show is. Basically, the attraction is a short stage show in which animatronic bears play instruments and sing. It's really that simple. A lot of people really like it for some reason, so take a chance and try it out for yourself. The wait time is rarely more than a few minutes long, so be sure to check it out when you're passing through Frontierland. Also, if you have kids, they'll probably enjoy the show even though it doesn't have any of the mainstream characters involved in it. You may be one of those guests that really likes the attraction and will never want it to go away.

Pecos Bill Tall Tale Inn and Cafe- A recently re-imagined menu for this dining location has just started being served in Frontierland. This new menu is supposed to be very good. The new options include various Texas inspired Mexican food dishes. When you order, don't worry about adding or changing your order to get what you want on it. When you get your food, it all comes plain and you get to take it over to a topping bar that has virtually anything you would want to put on Mexican food. If you don't want Mexican food, don't worry. They have a lot of other simpler options still available. Once you top your food, the seating area is fairly large and themed around an older style clay building that you could find in Mexico. There is plenty of seating most of the time, and you can sit and relax without having to worry about temperature or weather because it's nearly all indoor seating.

Golden Oak Outpost- If you're not looking for a full meal but more of a snack, take a few steps around the corner toward Fantasyland and check out Golden Oak Outpost. Fairly recently, the options here were also changed, but almost everyone agrees it was for the better. The only real menu items at this outdoor only food stand are waffle fries or sweet potato fries. You can get the standard french fries if you request it, but the draw to this food location is the fry toppings. You can get BLT or even barbecue pork topped fries. Both options are really tasty and you won't be disappointed. The price for these items does need to be mentioned though. For either of the fries, the cost is $7.99 and is a bit much for a cardboard tray full of french fries. In all honesty, Golden Oak Outpost successfully continues the trend at the Disney parks towards new, and distinct foods, but the prices definitely need some help.

Tom Sawyer Island- If you move over to the waters edge, be sure to check out Tom Sawyer Island. A lot of guests, and some of the most frequent guests never go over there. I think everyone should go at least once, even if it's just to ride the little raft over to the island. However, I would recommend doing more than just that. Take a walk down the many little trails and be on the lookout for hidden areas that are often looked right past. Most guests just walk the outside of the Island and completely overlook all that there is to do farther into it.

If you have kids, be sure to check out the second island as well. Yes, there is a second island that most overlook completely. Since nobody ever seems to go there, it is a great place to take kids with a lot of energy or just a good way to get away from the crowds in the rest of the park. There is actually a fort across the bridge that is a great place for kids to explore and to give you a break to sit down or even explore for yourself. With all of these little details mentioned, don't expect a lot of thrills on Tom Sawyer Island. It's still just a little area of land to explore. If you're lucky, you can get a little snack meal on the island, but the food location is rarely open and is used exclusively to sell peanut butter and jelly sandwiches most of the time. Walking around here is hard to explain, but to be honest, it may not be worth your time. It can be a fun place to go, but I wouldn't go as far as to say it should go on your list of must do's in the Magic Kingdom. Also, usually when you have some time to kill it isn't even open. The island is rarely open in the early mornings and is hardly ever open at night, so your only timeframe to go is usually in the heat of the afternoon.

Big Thunder Mountain Railroad- Don't let this attraction fool you. I have heard a few guests walk by the wait time for this attraction and say something like, "Why would I wait that long for the train, I can walk to the front of the park faster than that!" Yes, this is referred to as a railroad, but it is most definitely not the railroad that circles the park. It is actually one of the best thrill rides in all of the Disney parks and possibly one of the best family roller coasters ever built. Nearly everyone can enjoy this attraction. Even though the ride is based on the story of a runaway mine train, it's fast enough for the coaster lover, but slow enough that it doesn't really bother people that have queasy stomachs. My own dad, who can't ride in a car with anyone else because his motion sickness is so bad, can easily enjoy this attraction. It was hard to get him on it originally, but now it is one of his favorites. Even though it isn't all that fast, it is fairly jerky. Even though it sounds crazy, if you're worried about getting on this attraction, be sure to ride during the day. At night, the coaster becomes much more intense and actually is believed to get faster as the day progresses and the track heats up with constant use.

Overall, Thunder Mountain is one of the most heavily themed roller coasters you will ever find and it's just a bonus that all your friends and family can enjoy it, even if they don't really like roller coasters to begin with. Personally, I think it is the best attraction in the Magic Kingdom and the wait time usually reflects it. The average wait is usually near an hour, but it is definitely worth the extra time in line. Also worth mentioning is that the queue setup makes for probably the most uncomfortable wait of all the attractions. Once you get to the part of the queue inside the building, there is virtually no air conditioning and rarely even a slight breeze. That combination isn't the best for the Florida heat, but is well worth it to get to experience this wonderful attraction. That being said, definitely get a fastpass+ if you can.

The Frontierland Railroad Station- If you're looking for the actual railroad that circles the park, this is the train you want. As the most unique train station, being that it is basically on a second story, it's not something you want to miss. Additionally, you may want to actually use this station, because it is probably the most useful part of the railroad as actual transportation around the parks. Once you get back to Frontierland, it is a really long walk back to the front of the park, so why not ride the train? In the past, you used to be able to walk up and get on, but more recently there has been a pretty decent wait just to board in Frontierland. The other stations aren't usually as crowded, but it seems that more people are starting to utilize the train than they used to and the increased park attendance really doesn't help the situation. I should mention that during certain times of day such as parade times and while the Wishes nighttime fireworks show is going on, the trains will not run for a period of time for safety reasons. However, be sure to use the trains. They are quite a bit of fun to ride and save you a lot of time walking back and forth in the parks.

If you're like Walt Disney and are fascinated by steam engines, be sure to look into The Magic Behind Our Steam Trains Tour. On the tour, you get much closer to the trains and the engineers show you how every little aspect of the trains function. On top of that, you get to learn a little bit more about the backstory of the locomotives and even get to go behind the scenes to where the trains are stored each night. The best part is, once you get to the storage area, you get to see the monorails as well. The way the whole storage area is set up is that the trains are on the ground level and the monorails are on the "second floor" above you. It really is a great tour, and for someone who has been to Disney many times, it is a great way to experience something new and learn a little Disney history along the way!

ADVENTURELAND: There are very few parts of Disney World that Walt Disney has had more of a legacy built into than Adventureland. From the creation of the Enchanted Tiki Room to the rumors surrounding Pirates of the Caribbean, Walt's influence is in just about every detail. Even though his influence may not be obvious or stated directly, the backstory really makes the attractions special in many cases. Additionally, the area is undergoing a lot of changes that are creating new experiences every day. The changes haven't taken anything away, but rather added to the overall Adventureland design.

Swiss Family Tree House- As one of the simplest, yet most iconic attractions in the park, the Swiss Family Tree house is something a lot of guests can do without, but would never want to get rid of. It really has that nostalgia factor that makes it a timeless attraction. It's basically always been there and it's presence really helps define the theming for many returning guests. The experience is based off of a movie and book that I have never seen, but apparently features a family that lives in an elaborate treehouse. The whole attraction is basically a set of stairs that leads to the top of the tree and you get to see how the house functions up in the tree along the way.

To be honest, it's just a lot of stairs, but the views from the top are really unique and something that is worth seeing if you have the time. I really wish they could at least add a slide or something to make coming back down a little more interesting! However, it's hard to complain because the treehouse rarely has a wait time and if it does, just keep walking and do something else because there won't be one when you come back by. It is good to mention, this ride is not handicap accessible to my knowledge, so you will be required to walk up several flights of stairs if you wish to partake in the experience. Either way, it's definitely not a must do in the Magic Kingdom unless you just want something to do and to not have to wait to do it.

The Magic Carpets of Aladdin- The carpets are one of the more recent additions to the Adventureland area. Basically they're the same as Dumbo, but with a little twist. That twist comes in two ways that make the ride a little more interesting. The first of these is that the flying carpets each hold up to four guests per carpet as opposed to two. The riders in the front control the motion of the carpet up and down while those in the back use a button to tilt the carpet forward and backwards. With the ride vehicles covered, we can move on to the most enjoyable difference, the spitting camel. Yes, there is a spitting camel on the ride, but don't be alarmed. It's animatronic and it only spits water. Once you get in the air, it's incredibly entertaining to try to get the riders in your carpet wet as you fly past the camel. The spitting camel really turns the classic attraction into something new and interesting. Just like Dumbo, it's always fun for the whole family, but The Magic Carpets of Aladdin rarely have a wait time over half an hour and that's always a good thing at Walt Disney World.

Walt Disney's Enchanted Tiki Room- Just like other parts of the Magic Kingdom, including the Tomorrowland Speedway, this attraction originated in Anaheim at the Disneyland Resort. It was such a success when it was created in California that the Walt Disney Company decided to create a second edition in Disney World. The attraction itself also has a unique story behind it that is never advertised directly in the parks. In an original television program, Walt Disney debuted the animatronic birds for the Tiki Room and shocked the world. The Imagineers at Disney had created one of the first successful replications of animal life in the form of birds. Not only had they accomplished this, but they had also created an elaborate system that gave these animatronics the ability to perform in unison in a collaborative show that could be repeated many times. A version of that original show is still found in the Disney parks today, with the exception of a few new tweaks. The show has stood the test of time and become a true Disney classic in both Disneyland and Walt Disney World. No matter what your age or preferences, the Enchanted Tiki Room has a little something for everyone. As an added bonus, this is another attraction that rarely ever has a wait time greater than the time period before the next show begins. The show itself is only about 10 minutes long, so it is nearly always something you can do, even on the most crowded days in the Magic Kingdom.

Not surprisingly, that's not all the history the Enchanted Tiki Room has in store. At a recent Disney expo, Richard Sherman told a story about the attraction that really changed my views on the Enchanted Tiki Room altogether. In the story, he talked about his time with his brother Robert Sherman while working for Walt Disney and distinctly mentioned this attraction. After seeing the show for the first time, he told Walt that it was a great show, but that he really had no idea what it was. When he mentioned that, Walt Disney looked right at him and said that he wanted he and his brother to write a song that explained all that the show exhibited. As monumental as that task was, the result is the attraction that we still have today in not one, but two, locations. Beyond just this one influence, the Sherman brothers work can be found in many places across the parks and resorts, as well as in Mary Poppins, one of their most famous compositions. The Sherman brothers truly changed the parks forever, and influenced Disney in a way that can never really be fully understood. Imagine a park without music or the story of Marry Poppins without the wonderful songs. Nothing would be the same, and ultimately, we have these brothers to thank!

Jungle Cruise- As one of the few attractions that actually changes once a year, the Jungle Cruise has always been and always will be a classic. The reason I say it changes once a year is due to the fact that the Jungle Cruise transforms for a period of time each year into the Christmas themed "Jingle Cruise" for the enjoyment of the guests. The experience at this time of year is unique and very fun, but most of the time, the Jungle Cruise is set up in its standard way. In these cases, you take a slow moving boat ride through the jungle with a skipper that narrates your adventure in a fresh and comical way. There are a few surprises along the way, but, overall, it is a great family experience that most people enjoy. The best part is, you will never have the same experience twice with real cast members as skippers. However, due to its legacy as one of the earliest attractions in the Disney parks and its place as a family friendly attraction, the wait time often reaches well over 45 minutes. The good news is, usually you can catch a shorter wait if you keep coming back throughout the day.

Although not attached to the attraction directly, be on the lookout for the new dining location based on the Jungle Cruise, Skipper Canteen. The location has just opened, but features a series of dining rooms that expand the Jungle Cruise story. For all types of guests, this dining location is one to look forward to and I'm sure it will live up to expectations as Disney Imagineering almost always does. While early reports on food are really only starting to surface most people seem impressed. Even more are thrilled that at this time you can walk up and get a reservation opposed to booking online in advance. Skipper Canteen is the first of the table service restaurants to go back to this seating style, so it could be a test or maybe even a nod to what's coming back in the future.

Pirates of the Caribbean- Just as many of the attractions in Adventureland, Pirates of the Caribbean is also a classic, iconic, attraction. Pirates really takes the idea of a "Disney classic" to a whole new level. Despite all of the various changes over the years, the attraction has always held on to what has made it so incredibly successful. There's just something about coming to Walt Disney World to ride Pirates of the Caribbean that puts a smile on your face. In a similar way to "it's a small world", you have to ride it whenever you're in Walt Disney World. Pirates, no matter how simple, strikes a balance between adventure and family orientation that very few attractions can accomplish.

Anyone can get on the attraction and have a good time, but in a way, this is what started that trend in all other Disney attractions. How many attractions in the Magic Kingdom aren't suitable for families? The answer is simple: very, very, few. In my opinion, it's better off that way. You see, attractions like Pirates bring families together and really let you have an experience that you will remember. All too often, families go to amusement parks and split up and do what they each consider fun. Disney creates incredible entertainment, but do it in a way that you can all experience things together. This concept is one of the many things that really sets Disney apart.

In regards to the attraction itself, there is one "thrill" aspect of the ride in the way of a small hill. It kind of sneaks up on you if you're not paying attention. It may shock you the first time, but it pails in comparison to any of the hills found on Splash Mountain. In all reality, you can't go wrong with Pirates of the Caribbean. Unfortunately, as with many elements of Disney, a unique rumor surrounds Pirates. The rumor goes beyond the attraction, quite literally. In the past many believed that Walt Disney had his head cryogenically frozen in order to have the ability to come back in the case that the possibility would arise through robotic technology. The frozen head is believed to be stored under Pirates of the Caribbean. According to legend, this is true, but in reality and in historical records, Walt Disney was actually cremated. Surprisingly, this has never been publicly confirmed, but rather just accepted by a majority of people. The story adds a little something extra to a beloved attraction of nearly all Disney guests, but it is a little interesting that Disney has never proved that it is not true.

Tortuga Tavern- I'll be completely honest with you about this dining location. The likelihood of it actually being open while you're in the area is extremely rare. I am not quite sure why this is, but in the extremely numerous times I have been in the Magic Kingdom, I can only recall it being open one time.

One reason for this could be the fact that the food offerings are very similar to those around the corner at Pecos Bill's. From my experience, no one really knows why it's never open other than it is a seasonal location. The Disney description of seasonal here doesn't quite make sense, because I was recently in the parks for New Years (one of the busiest days of the year) and I don't believe it was even open on that day. That being said, I can't blame Disney for not having it open because, it really isn't needed with another Mexican-style restaurant literally attached to the back side of this location. That being said, if you're in the area and for some reason it is open be sure to check it out. You never know when you'll get the chance to eat there again.

Sunshine Tree Terrace- The Magic Kingdom has two incredibly unique ice cream style desserts that you can't find anywhere else. The Terrace is one of these locations and the other is Aloha Isle. At the Terrace, be sure to try the citrus swirl. It definitely won't disappoint the taste buds, and you can only get this delightful dessert at one location in the parks. As a part of a recent change, Sunshine Tree Terrace has actually switched locations with Aloha Isle. If you're a returning guest, don't be alarmed. It is still the same menu at both locations, but they swapped physical counters due to popularity in an effort to manage crowds.

Aloha Isle- The other exclusive dessert of the Magic Kingdom actually isn't as exclusive as it once was. The pineapple Dole Whip found at Aloha Isle is something that has to be tried in order to fully understand its reputation. Unlike most ice cream, Dole Whip has a unique consistency that is more of a juice rather than a cream base. As a result, it makes for a flavor and texture that can never be rivaled. Personally, I overlooked this amazing treat for years. Now, I get one nearly ever time I am in the Magic Kingdom. It really is that good.

Fortunately, now you don't even have to be in the park to try this tasty treat. With the recent redesign of the Polynesian Village Resort, a new location was also debuted named Pineapple Lanai. At the back of the lobby, go through the back doors and directly to your left will be Pineapple Lanai's walk up counter. As the fourth location nationwide, it is also the only Disney location that is outside of a theme park. At the Hawaii Dole Plantation, you can also get Dole Whip, but it isn't quite the same and isn't even called Dole Whip. The Dole Company owns the rights to the name, so they got to call it what they wished at their own location. As for the Disney locations, this iconic dessert is actually not your only option. Additionally, Aloha Isle sells a Dole Whip float as well as fresh pineapple. Even though it isn't quite as exclusive as it once was, be sure to try a Dole Whip next time you're at or near the Magic Kingdom. You definitely will not regret it!

With nearly all there is to do in the Magic Kingdom covered, you can really see how special and magical of a place it truly is. It's not at all hard to believe why this park is so close to so many guest's hearts. The memories created here are priceless and cannot be matched by any other vacation destination. The first time I went into the Magic Kingdom as a kid, I had no idea I would be writing this book and really never expected that people would ever be reading anything that I wrote. It's amazing how something as simple as a vacation destination can change the way you live your life. My family never expected to be the type of people that go to Disney World every year, but it has a way of drawing you back through memories and experiences that you will always have and cherish.

A lot of people see a number when they go to the Disney parks and think, "Wow, that can't be worth it!" and never give it a chance. If you don't listen to anything else I say in this book, be sure to remember this. Yes, the parks are incredibly expensive, but what isn't these days? I've heard stories from hundreds of people that say Disney gave them an experience of a lifetime, and you can't put a price on that. There are a lot of options available to make the experience more economical, but I can never guarantee that your vacation will be cheap. Fortunately, what I can guarantee, is that you will remember it forever and enjoy nearly every moment if you keep the reason for going in the first place in the back of your mind. Don't go for the attractions and don't go for the food, go for the experiences that you'll never get to have again, and the Magic Kingdom is an incredible place to start.

DISNEY'S EPCOT CENTER

-Above: Spaceship Earth

Epcot Center is one of those parks that either you love it or you hate it. In my opinion, the people who hate it aren't doing something right. Epcot has a little bit of everything. Up front, you have nearly all of your attractions, and then as you move deeper into the parks, you find one of the most unique concepts in theme park history, the World Showcase. Although the park isn't filled with wall to wall attractions, there is so much to experience that you can never quite do it all. In this section of the book, we will try to cover the main points of the park, but, in reality, you can never cover all that Epcot Center has to offer. From the attractions and dining, to the two major festivals held there each year, the park is always changing and always a good place to explore time after time.

You may have noticed that on a majority of current Disney websites and even in the park itself, it is often labeled simply as Epcot. I have avoided that shortened version of Epcot Center for a reason. Originally, the park was known as Epcot Center, and that is truly what the design by Walt Disney called for. It would be an Experimental Prototype Community of Tomorrow. A center for entertainment and housing that was to be the model city of the future. Sadly, these plans were scaled down after Walt Disney passed away before his dream could become a reality. He had everything planned and even released a television program based on the idea. When the driving force behind the project disappeared with Walt Disney, the goal of Epcot became redirected into a similar design that is found in the park today. That Epcot Center name is really all that remained the same and, in a way, I've never wanted that vision to be completely forgotten. The name always saved the legacy of Walt Disney and was really the only true element of the park that remained completely original to the plans for many years.

FUTURE WORLD: As the first section of the park, and the closest in relation to the original project design, Future World fills a unique spot in the Disney parks. Apart from Innoventions and Spaceship Earth, the area is divided into Future World East and West. Each of these two areas have a common theme of invention and new ways of doing things, but are separated in their goals. Future World West encompasses imagination and new creations in nature and science. Future World East focuses primarily on new technologies and steps being taken in the industrial world. Each portion has a unique history that is often overlooked, but has ultimately developed them into what they have become today. With the set up out of the way, we'll start with the attractions that are front and center and then move on first to Future World West, followed by East.

THE "MAIN STREET": There really is no term for this area so that's the best we have to work with. If you're coming from the main entrance, you can't miss these attractions, so don't worry about having to look too hard for them. On most park maps over the years they have decided to call these attractions a part of Future World East, but they aren't really in that designated area, nor do they really fit with that theming.

Spaceship Earth- When you first walk into the park, there is no possible way to overlook Spaceship Earth. As the parks icon, everyone wants to ride whatever is inside of the enormous geodesic dome. Due to the fact that it is the first attraction you come to in the park, many first time guests get in line for it first thing in the morning. I am positive this is never the best option. When the park opens, you are much better off going to either Soarin' or Test Track and then circling back to Spaceship Earth later in the day. At night, especially, the attraction has a much shorter wait time than during the day. Whenever you do decide to ride, be sure to know what you're getting into and manage your expectations accordingly.

Many people see the design of Spaceship Earth and automatically assume it must be a roller coaster. It is definitely not a roller coaster, and actually quite the opposite. The attraction is built on a track that slowly rotates the ride vehicles to the top of the sphere, then back down. Along the way, there are a series of various rooms representing technological improvements over the years. The attraction is entertaining for certain people, but others find it quite boring. Once you get to the top though, it really comes alive. As you enter this large dome shaped room, you get to see your spaceship, Earth, from space.

The whole experience really forces you to think about the realities of technology and one of the most unique parts of the attraction is a direct result of modern technology itself. Once the vehicle turns around and prepares for descent, be sure to shut your eyes, and you won't be disappointed when you open them. As the first room of the descent gets close, open your eyes and you will be stunned by an amazing illusion created by hundreds of led lights. To be honest, these two rooms are really the highlight of the entire attraction.

Once you get all the way back down, you will have been on a journey through the ages and will inevitably be inspired for the future. With the attraction being simple and straightforward, it isn't always one that everyone loves. That being said, it's hard to pass up a ride on Spaceship Earth. It is one of Disney's classic icons and the only one that an attraction actually exists within.

Innoventions East and West- Innoventions West is actually currently being redesigned for a future expansion with the exception of the character spot near by, and a simple seating area for charging cell phones. Even though the details for the redesign have not been officially released, Disney has said that it will be something new and different than the past. As for Innoventions East, it is actually home to the newest edition to Epcot Center. The area itself is a series of games and interactive experiences that are all housed in an indoor area. None of these experience are too terribly exciting, but can be a lot of fun for kids and a great place to take a break from the heat and other elements.

The newest edition to the East side is an experience sponsored by Glidden Paints that allows the guest to create various paint colors using a series of levers and wheels. Additionally, the new experience features a 30 minute film and even an area to use a magic paintbrush to create a digital masterpiece. For adults, this probably won't be the most interesting experience, but most kids will love the hands on activities. As mentioned before, Innoventions has a lot of unique opportunities, but they've been known to change fairly frequently over the years. There is even rumor that they could be going away completely in the near future!

FUTURE WORLD WEST:

Epcot Character Spot- Although this isn't necessarily an attraction, the Character Spot is often overlooked in Future World. It is a simple location where you and your friends or family can meet a variety of characters which almost always include the classic characters with special backdrops. The location is possibly one of the best places to get the most character interaction all in one place. Kids really love the Character Spot and it is a great way to avoid the ridiculously long lines that form when a character shows up in the parks somewhere. More recently, and possibly only for a limited time, you can even meet Baymax from Big Hero 6. The meet and great was relocated after the development of Star Wars Launch Bay began at Hollywood Studios, but it was probably for the better. At it's new location, there is a more elaborate backdrop and the overall character interaction is much better than it was in the previous location.

The Seas With Nemo And Friends- Nemo and Friends is an extremely simple attraction, and one that usually has a very short wait time. Once you enter the attraction's queue, you are transported under the sea. After walking through a maze of a queue area you board your clam shell vehicle and join Dory and Marlin as they go on an adventure to find Nemo. Within the clam shell, you get to be part of a comical recreation of your favorite scenes found in the movie. For example, many guests really enjoy the part of the attraction that puts you in the EAC, or East Australian Current, and it is really one of the highlights of your journey.

Near the end of the ride is where it really starts to come alive, and quite literally! As your journey comes to an end, the projections that make up the entire attraction transfer onto a real-life aquarium with actual aquatic life. That trend continues into the post show area which is quite similar to how the attraction used to be when it was The Living Seas.

The post-attraction is filled with large fish, dolphins, manatees, and even some sharks and stingrays. It's almost as if you can experience a full fledge aquarium in a theme park. Additionally, scattered around the area are experts that work with the animals each and every day to run tests and improve their quality of life while scientists learn more about the animals. Be sure to take a moment to ask a few questions about the animals, because these cast members really know their stuff.

The last time I was at the The Seas With Nemo And Friends, it was feeding time and we got to witness one of the rarest stingrays found in the world. Disney had one on site to help protect and learn about the species. While we were there, the divers were performing a training exercise with the animal and a wonderful cast member said to ask any questions we wanted. We asked a few questions and she made sure to answer every one of them in great detail due to the fact that she had worked with the animal personally in the past. You can't even find that kind of service in a full-fledge aquarium and Disney offers it at no additional charge! The attraction leading up to this isn't too terribly impressive, so it is often overlooked. I have never really been a fan of the Nemo attraction, but you can always skip it if you really don't wish to utilize your time in that particular way. Even if you choose to skip the actual Nemo experience, be sure to go in the "exit" and at least check out all the aquariums have in store for each and every guest. Although it isn't really marked, you can always wander in the gift shop at the end of the attraction and keep going on into the aquarium areas, even if you didn't ride the attraction.

Turtle Talk With Crush- Within the aquarium area listed above, Turtle Talk with Crush allows guests of all ages to interact with Crush from the Finding Nemo movie. As an onscreen, character based show, Crush talks and answers questions live and in person. Surprisingly, on occasion, this attraction can get quite crowded. Given the goal of the show, it is almost exclusively for kids or families with kids. As with everything at Disney, they are never going to turn adults away, but it may not be too terribly interesting for a majority of older guests. For the younger guests though, Turtle Talk With Crush has almost unlimited repeat value. The show is rarely the same twice, so you can always go back time after time if you would like.

Coral Reef Restaurant- Just outside of The Seas is a hard to find seafood restaurant that really puts you in the middle of a coral reef. Attached to one side of The Seas pavilion, the dining room is surrounded by real aquatic life. As one of the lesser known Epcot dining locations, the Coral Reef seems to be a little less popular than most table service locations. As with all dining locations in the Disney parks that aren't as mainstream, getting reservations can be much less difficult and definitely less tiresome.

The menu here features various seafood dishes that often have a unique take on a classic item. Unfortunately, I have never had the opportunity to dine at this location, but have heard many stories about how good the food really is. The location itself is semi-upscale and the menu prices do reflect it. The dining area itself successfully creates a feeling of being underwater and really immerses you in the aquatic theming that allows the restaurant to live up to its name. Due to the theming and not so much the menu offerings, this can be a location for families, but focuses on some not so kid-friendly menu items, unless your child is more adventurous than most. The Coral Reef is definitely on my list of things to do at Walt Disney World, so I encourage you to try this unique Disney dining location as well.

Soarin'- Moving on to one of the most popular attractions in Disney history, Soarin' has always blown away every guest's expectations. Going into the attraction, you can't really get a grasp of what to expect until you experience it for yourself. Soarin' takes a motion theatre to the next level. As you enter the theatre, you are met with a distinct fragrance that lets you know something special is about to happen, and surprisingly you will never forget that aroma even after leaving the attraction.

Once you take your seat on a uniquely designed hanging bench that mimics a hang glider, you are faced with a one of a kind sensation. The bench sways ever so gently, then once everyone is buckled in and ready to go the entire row lifts and places you right in the middle of a gigantic curved screen. Once you're in the air, the screen comes to life and projects a series of different scenarios giving the illusion of flying. At the same time your bench mimics a hang glider and shifts in the breeze as various accompanying scents blow gently into your face. When all of those sensory elements come together, the experience is incomparable and incredibly realistic.

A lot of guests worry about Soarin' when they ride for the first time due to the motion theatre aspect. I was one of those people until I tried it. I have struggled with motion sickness on attractions similar to this for years, but I have never had the slightest problem during this experience. As a piece of advice for these type of people and the best advice I received before riding Soarin' is quite simple: If you start to feel uncomfortable, just close your eyes. The motion, once taken away from the projected movie, is no different or more severe than being in a rocking chair.

On the other hand, if you are afraid of heights, I would not get on this ride! In every row, no matter if you are in the front or the back, you will be lifted off of the ground a pretty good piece, and it can definitely be a little unnerving if you do not like heights. While taking all that into consideration, be sure to take a chance with this attraction, because it is truly amazing to experience. Due to the one of a kind nature of Soarin', the wait time is often well over two hours long. Be sure to get there early in the morning or schedule a fastpass+ to avoid the crowds. It is definitely a must-ride in Epcot Center.

The attraction is undergoing a big change throughout part of 2016. For a while, a new film for Soarin' has been rumored, but Disney has officially released that the new film is coming. The updated attraction will have the same design and on-ride experience, but the film will feature places around the world rather than just California. In conjunction with the film, Soarin' will actually feature a higher quality screen and many assume a higher quality projection as well. Even though both of these are good additions, the best addition actually comes in the way of a third theatre. We can only assume that the new theatre will further spread out the line queue and shrink the wait times. Disney has not officially released if one theatre will become fastpass+ only or not, but it can be assumed that they will attempt to shrink the wait times in any way they can. As one of the most popular attractions, it is a long overdue expansion.

Living with the Land- Once you leave Soarin', try not to overlook this little boat ride across the way. Living with the Land is a very simple ride through a few scenes that tell a story of how to live with the land in order to meet the needs of society. The most intriguing aspect of the attraction is a journey through Disney's onsite greenhouses. Each house provides for various restaurants on property, including Garden Grill, directly above the entrance to Living with the Land.

As for the greenhouses themselves, they are like nothing you have ever seen or will ever see again. All of the plants are grown in incredibly strange, but incredibly successful ways. They really have a little bit of everything. From aquaculture to hydroponics, if you can't find a state of the art growing technology here, you will not find it anywhere else in the world. Once the attraction finishes, there is a tour that you can take for an additional fee if you desire to get a closer look at all there is to offer.

Living with the Land is one of those rare remaining hidden gems of the parks. The majority of guests don't have any idea how entertaining this attraction can be and simply skip right over it. Since so many people just ignore it, the wait time is almost always non existent and a great, simple, attraction that you don't want to miss. Sadly, it has also changed slightly over the years. If you have had the opportunity to ride it in the past, the name may sound familiar, but it is not quite the same. Many years ago, the attraction underwent a slight remodel of sorts which removed the original Listen to the Land soundtrack and updated the name to Living with the Land. Luckily the attraction remained mainly the same and the original soundtrack is readily available online, even today!

The Circle of Life- Although this is more of a simple movie rather than a full fledge attraction, some people could really enjoy it. It is basically a conservation film with Timon and Pumbaa from the Lion King movies. The movie itself is fairly long and hardly ever has a wait. To be honest, that's probably for a reason. The attraction isn't all that interesting and unless you have an abundance of extra time, I would say just to skip over The Circle of Life. I won't say that very often, but I think I have only ever seen the show once, and it was pretty forgettable. If I didn't have a map in front of me, I probably would have forgotten all about this attraction.

Captain EO- Captain EO has just recently ended its second run in Epcot Center. The show which will be the replacement is based on Disney short films. As a fan of the Disney shorts, I'm really looking forward to this attraction and it should bring something new and exciting to Epcot. Before Captain EO, some Disney guests may remember Honey I Shrunk the Audience. This show was one of the longer lasting ones that has been in this location, but it was replaced with Captain EO's second run in the parks. As you can see, the theatre itself has been a variety of different things and nothing has really lasted for a significant period of time in that location. Be aware, the short films in this theatre could last 5 years or it could last 2 months. With Disney and this location, there really is no way to tell for sure.

Journey Into Imagination With Figment- If there was a definition of a feel-good attraction, this would be it. Journey Into Imagination has always been a childhood favorite of mine, so I can be a little biased when talking about it. For me, there is so much to like about the attraction, no matter how simple it really is. You enter the attraction and board a tram that will take you through a series of sensory labs with Dr. Nigel Channing as your guide. I know it sounds crazy, but it really is a fun attraction that you can almost always walk right up and get on. The kicker to Journey Into Imagination comes at the very beginning of the journey when you are introduced to Figment, the figment of the imagination.

Figment is a purple dragon that flies and embodies everything found in your imagination. He's everything we love about life and the Disney parks all rolled into one character. Once he shows up in the attraction, it takes a turn for the silly and the Doctor loses control of his friend, Figment. Without spoiling any secrets, the ride really ends with a BLAST! Sadly, despite its draw with virtually any audience, there has been rumors for years that it could be going away in the near future. Although I hope this is not the case, it probably will become a reality sooner rather than later. Given that this is the third design of an attraction that debuted many years ago with a slightly different storyline, it is unlikely to be redesigned again, but rather replaced. As unfortunate as this is, be sure to get in a ride to at least say you got a chance to ride Journey Into Imagination with Figment.

There are a few rumors floating around that the original theming will make a return to the attraction. Sadly, this is probably more rumor than reality, but we can only wish that it will really come to fruition! In addition, Disney Vacation Club members have been almost guaranteed that upstairs ImageWorks will reopen as a DVC lounge. I'm not positive, but if that is the case, we can only assume that Disney will be doing something to liven up the attraction rather than get rid of it. I couldn't be more excited if that ends up being the case!

ImageWorks- At the end of the Journey Into Imagination attraction is ImageWorks. This area, which once filled two stories with unique, hands on, experiences has dwindled to a small section of a few interactive exhibits upon leaving Journey Into Imagination. At one point this was a beautiful location, especially once you reached the upstairs area. Today it is honestly a little sad and only a few people exiting the ride are ever actually interacting with the few exhibits left. Hopefully, ImageWorks will get a redesign in the near future and transition into the latest and greatest aspect of Epcot Center.

Club Cool- As a crossover between a snack location and an attraction, Club Cool fills a sort of niche in Epcot. It isn't quite an attraction, and it isn't quite a full-scale dining location. You walk into the building and Coca-Cola has a series of sponsored vending machines. The machines don't have the standard flavors Coca-Cola provides in the United States, but rather various drinks found around the world. Surprisingly, since this is Disney World, these drinks are actually free. The goal of the experience is to try the sodas from around the world and find a favorite, but most of the drinks actually taste pretty terrible. If you're looking for a more classic experience and a real drink, they are also available, but you do have to pay for them. Club Cool is a pretty neat little area, but not something that is going to take up much time on your vacation. The experience and the look on your friends face when they try a terrible flavor, may just give you a memory that could be a highlight of your day at Epcot! You never know what can leave an impression on your vacation, so be sure to take a few minutes and enjoy Club Cool on your way to the World Showcase.

Fountain View- Recently in the Epcot park as well as all the other parks, a location serving a select few Starbucks drinks have appeared. The partnership faced a lot of controversy, especially in the Magic Kingdom, but overall a lot of guests are enjoying the change. In Epcot, this is your location to find Starbucks, but additionally they serve a few breakfast sandwiches and pastries. As with any pastries, but especially Disney pastries, the food is quite good and a great place to grab a quick breakfast in the park.

Sunshine Seasons- If you are looking for a different meal, Sunshine Seasons offers lunch and dinner, each with a variety of good offerings in the way of soups, salads, and sandwiches. Nearly everything they have to offer is fresh and a good portion of the menu is seasonal. Partly because of its location near Soarin' and The Land, Seasons is often overlooked. As a result, it isn't normally as crowded as other dining locations. To be honest, I don't usually eat at this location unless it is for breakfast, because the World Showcase has so many great dining options. Unfortunately, Disney has stopped serving breakfast here and now serves breakfast at Garden Grill instead. However, if you're in the Future World area and looking for a good meal be sure to try Sunshine Seasons.

The Garden Grill- Over the years, this table service dining location in the Land Pavilion has undergone multiple menu alterations. The original menu was great and the food was incredible, so it was always a must-do dining location for our family. The atmosphere alone made the restaurant worth going to, and the food was just a great bonus. Garden Grill itself is actually a circular, constantly revolving, seating area that mesmerizes guests time after time. As the floor slowly rotates but the encompassing building stays stationary, you get to see every part of the restaurant without leaving your seat. As the dining area spins at a very slow pace, you not only get to see around the room, but can also view sections of Living with the Land from above.

Once you get your food, the meal is a family style dining experience. Your server brings one of everything to your table and you can always ask for more of any item you choose. The items on the menu change, but a staple is usually some type of flank steak and a chicken dish of some sort. The food has always been pretty good, but the price for the dining experience continues to climb and the food quality tends to remain the same. For those of you who love a good character meal, this has always been a great option. Chip and Dale are always ready to interact with your table and they always have some friends along with them as well. Garden Grill is a fun experience and one that I have always enjoyed, but with so many great dining options in Epcot Center, there is almost always a better dining reservation to be had at a comparable price point.

FUTURE WORLD EAST:

Ellen's Energy Adventure- The Energy Adventure in my opinion is an attraction that is past it's prime for a variety of reasons. The idea in theory is great, but the attraction no longer draws crowds and takes up a huge amount of time just to go through. When you board the ride, you do so in a similar way that you do the Great Movie Ride at Hollywood Studios. The vehicle is very large and accommodates quite a few guests at a time as a sort of theatre on wheels. Once you're seated, be prepared to be there for quite a while. To be almost exact, the entire Universe of Energy experience takes near 45 minutes to complete!

The attraction itself is a journey through time with Ellen DeGeneres as one of your guides on screen. The attraction is semi-entertaining at best, but to be fair, some people do enjoy it. To me, it's not worth your time in the parks and the space could be used for a new, more modern, attraction. If you have a big break in the day, you could check it out, but it never usually has a wait, so don't worry about rushing over to Ellen's Energy Adventure.

Mission: Space- The Mission Space attraction is one that many guests have mixed opinions of for a variety of reasons. Originally, when this attraction was built, it replaced Horizons. Horizons was a classic attraction in the Epcot theme park. The rumors surrounding its closure really caused a lot of unnecessary hard feelings towards Mission Space as it's replacement. When Horizons closed, rumors exploded everywhere because Disney never officially declared a reasonable explanation for it's closure. Disney's simple press release stated that one of the major reasons was decreased attraction popularity. Sadly, this was a pretty controversial statement, because the attraction was actually fairly popular. Shortly after the statement by Disney, pictures surfaced of a supposed sinkhole on the property very close to the backside of the building. Today, this seems to be the more accepted reason for Horizons closure due to the fact that the building itself had appeared to have sunk into the ground a decent amount after its de-construction was complete. Horizons is gone today, but sort of never forgotten. In the current Mission Space attraction, there are a few nods to the original Horizons logo that help keep the attractions' memory alive.

A second reason this attraction often has mixed opinions from guests is that it is one of the most intense attractions out of all of the Disney parks. Part of the issue is that it is essentially a high quality space-flight simulator, but that isn't necessarily the whole story. When the attraction opened, there was only one intensity level and a majority of guests could not handle the spinning and g-forces the spinning created. As a result, many guests got sick on the ride, which led to the addition of air sickness bags in the attraction vehicles. After creating this simple "fix" of sorts, Disney finally realized that if they wanted guests to enjoy the ride, they should offer two different intensities.

Today, there is an orange team option for the original experience or a green team option for a much less intense experience. Personally, if you decide to even attempt to ride this attraction, I cannot recommend it highly enough that you try the green team first. If you enjoy the attraction and think you can handle it, then go back and try the other version. The ride vehicles themselves are small pods in a circle around a centrifuge. As the pods spin at a very high speed it gives the feeling of intense g-forces on your body. Additionally, while spinning, the actual pod itself tilts and shakes to simulate movements of your ship. Throughout the entire process, you watch a screen that acts as your window in the spaceship. Each guest in your "crew" has an assigned roll and a series of buttons to initiate throughout your journey to Mars. Mars is the end destination of your flight, but the attraction itself covers a simulated experience of takeoff, flight, and even a crash landing.

Ultimately, Mission Space makes for an incredible and riveting experience, but be aware of any medical conditions or motion sickness problems you may have before you partake in the attraction. Disney has had several issues due to people not listening to the attractions posted warnings and recommendations. Some people really just should not get on this attraction. It can scare kids and potentially hurt anyone who is not in good health. That being said, the attraction is incredibly safe as long as the intended audience is who chooses to partake in the experience.

Test Track- Presented by Chevrolet- After World of Motion closed, a new attraction was needed. Test Track fit the bill perfectly. Originally, the attraction featured a crash test style experience of what a production vehicle underwent before reaching the consumer market. Recently, it underwent a huge design change which altered every aspect of the ride experience except the track itself. After the remodel, the attraction transitioned from the standard test scenario theme to a much more modern, almost futuristic, version of the same process. Additionally, there was a huge addition to the pre-show by way of a create-your-own vehicle design room.

Before boarding the attraction itself, you enter a special room of a series of very large touchscreens and design your own vehicle to test in the sim car. After creating your vehicle on-screen, the design follows you onto the track and displays your vehicles' performance throughout the environment on various screens. Once your experience on the track is over, you can interact with your design and see how it stacks up with the rest of the days' riders designs.

As for the attraction itself, it is actually one a majority of guests can really enjoy. You board a sim car with five other people to journey through simulated test phases. The look and feel of the attraction mimics a Tron style design. The tests included are everything from handling to economy ratings to even a high speed loop around the exterior of the building with a series of banked turns. A majority of the attraction features slower speeds, but the top speed in the outdoor section is near 62 mph. It really isn't for the faint of heart, but there is no upside down section or anything of that sort. By excluding these elements, it appeals more to a family audience.

As I mentioned, Test Track isn't for the faint of heart, but it really is a great experience to have with family, especially as you burst into laughter when you see your picture that was taken at top speed. I would go as far to say that if you think you can handle this attraction, there is virtually no chance you will leave without a smile on your face. One problem that arises with such an enjoyable ride is the sometimes outrageous wait time. If you don't want to wait, be sure to grab this attraction on your fastpass+, but be aware, you cannot pick both Soarin' and Test Track on your fastpass+ selections.

To remedy this situation the weird current system creates, I would suggest getting a fastpass+ for Test Track and going to Soarin' as soon as the park opens to avoid the long wait times at both attractions. I recommend this for a reason other than the reality that Test Track is my favorite attraction. Test Track is known to have simple malfunctions from time to time delaying the attractions' morning opening. None of these issues are ever big problems, but if you have a fastpass+ it will be honored at another time if the attraction is closed in this type of a situation. Somehow, no matter how long the wait is, be sure to ride Test Track. I can virtually guarantee you won't regret it.

Electric Umbrella- As the only counter service location in this corner of the park, with the exception of a fairly new grilled cheese truck, the Electric Umbrella offers a simple dining experience. The restaurant is based on a futuristic design full of bright lights and legitimate electric umbrellas. The food here is good, but very simple. The menu items include your standard amusement park burgers and chicken, but the chicken nuggets are actually really good. They are basically a little chicken finger as long as Disney hasn't randomly changed them.

As one of the very few restaurants you can get more common, American food in Epcot Center, it is a very popular location. The lines here aren't too bad, and there is a lot of seating, so the crowds are never really a big problem. Unfortunately, I can't really recommend this restaurant for a couple of reasons. The first is that the World Showcase offers so many great counter service locations that are so much more interesting and better overall than this location. The second reason is that there is nothing too special about the Electric Umbrella. The food is good, but not great, and you can get a much better dining experience than this at virtually any other Disney dining location in Epcot. When you think about it, we go to the parks for unique experiences and eating chicken nuggets and hamburgers can be done anywhere. Unless you have an extremely picky child, which is understandable, be sure to explore some of the countries in the World Showcase and try out one of the many dining options it offers instead of Electric Umbrella.

WORLD SHOWCASE: The World Showcase is potentially one of the most unique and enjoyable experiences in all of Walt Disney World. Although there is really only one attraction open currently, there is one in the works and possibly more to come. Attractions in the World Showcase were never really part of the original plan, but their addition has made the experience a little more immersive.

For those of you who don't know, the showcase itself is Disney's incredibly accurate recreation of the cultures and customs found in 11 countries around the world. Originally these areas were sponsored, for lack of a better word, by their actual countries and the countries themselves got to choose how they were represented. Currently that is no longer the case, despite popular belief. Disney phased out that program slowly over the years and today a couple of the countries represented are becoming a little controversial.

When we look at the countries in particular you'll see how they have changed and adopted slight variations over the years. Even from the very beginning, there were changes before the park was even built. Originally, there were plans for an Africa pavilion in addition to the other 11 countries. (There were actually 9 originally, then Morocco and Norway were added later on.) After the idea was scrapped, many believe it developed into the modern creation of Animal Kingdom. Even though Disney never confirmed this idea, it is commonly accepted today due to the fact that Africa is currently a huge part of the Animal Kingdom park. The parks are always changing and this example, in Epcot Center, is just one of the many changes that developed the park into what it is today.

The best and potentially most helpful tip I could give about the World Showcase is to try it for the first time starting in Canada, working your way around the lake counter clockwise. By doing this, you avoid a majority of the morning crowds because for some reason everyone feels the need to go the opposite direction around the lake. I know that sounds like a strange tip, but it makes a big difference. The crowds are much less overwhelming most of the time going "backwards", and it makes for a more enjoyable experience. Unfortunately, the crowds pick up in the afternoons, but I believe counter clockwise is always the best way to go. A second simple tip is to pick up a time guide when you enter the parks and look for all of the little shows that are found across the World Showcase. Many of them are extremely entertaining and you won't want to miss out. With those simple ideas covered, we'll get into more detail for each country represented.

Refreshment Port- Before you even get to the countries of the World Showcase, be sure to check out the Refreshment Port to start off your long journey around the lake with a snack. Here you can get a few items to eat, but the main offerings are frozen drinks and ice cream. Additionally, you can try one of the most unique and modern creations that can only be found in a few locations across the nation. This delightful dessert is termed the Croissant Donut or "Cronut". A Cronut is a little hard to explain, but it's basically a flakey donut that is coated in cinnamon sugar. Although it sounds strange, I can tell you from personal experience, it is an incredible dessert. Once you grab your Cronut or other snack item, head on over to the first country in the World Showcase, Canada.

Canada- For years, when I got to the Canada pavilion, I just walked right past it and never took the time to look around. Part of the reason I usually did this was that after walking the World Showcase from the other direction, I was normally tired of walking. By starting at Canada, you get to experience this area more fully and once you get to Mexico, you can look forward to a simple boat ride and plenty of places to relax at the end of your long journey. We'll get a little more in detail on Mexico in another section, but Canada has a lot to offer for such a small area.

For a small pavilion, it is potentially one of the best places to eat in all of the World Showcase. The table service location here is extremely hard to beat in both quality and atmosphere. The restaurant is named Le Cellier and is one of the best places to order steak across the entire Disney property. If you get the opportunity to dine here, you can't go wrong with the filet and the mashed potatoes. They are some of the best I've ever eaten. If you aren't a steak person, Le Cellier also offers a few seafood dishes that are equally as good, if not better than the steak. In addition to main entrees, the desserts and wine choices here are also fairly diverse and help create a draw for virtually any audience. Originally, this location was not a signature dining location for the standard dining plan, but its incredible popularity forced it into one in order to manage the reservations. Basically, what that means is that on the dining plan, if you choose to eat here, it will require two table service credits per person. Disney's plan to manage crowds by putting this in place worked flawlessly, but it is hard to pass up on another meal to use two credits for Le Cellier.

The only attraction in this area is in the form of a 14 minute show. The experience is called O Canada! and gives a brief look into the Canadian lifestyle through an exclusively Disney platform. The film is in what is called Circle Vision 360. In normal terms, that means the theater itself surrounds the audience on all sides as the name implies. It sounds simple, but it's pretty interesting in practice. After you finish, be sure to take a look around the gardens and other areas of the pavilion before moving on. The area is one of the more scenic of all the pavilions, no matter how small it is in comparison.

United Kingdom- As you keep on making your way around the World Showcase, you'll notice one country that is a little different from the rest. The area functions as a little British village that actually surrounds you as you follow the main path around the showcase. This simple difference sets the United Kingdom pavilion apart from all the others. Additionally, there a few little creative aspects that make it not only unique to Epcot, but unique from the rest of the world, quite literally. I know this sounds a little over exaggerated for a Disney pavilion, but the statement is a completely honest assessment. There are a few items in the shops of the United Kingdom that can only be found in Epcot and Buckingham Palace. It doesn't get much more true to the country itself than that.

Even beyond the simple items in the stores, there are a few experiences that really immerse you in the pavilions' theming. One of these is in the way of an exclusive event during the Christmas season. Throughout the fall and on into the beginning of winter, be sure to keep an eye out for the United Kingdom's version of Santa Clause, known as Father Christmas. As a much less modernized view of the character, it is great to hear him sing and to watch his interaction with guests of all ages. The wonderful outfit he wears is a traditional representation of the character and the actual story he tells of the holiday season is something you won't want to miss.

As for the dining, you can't go wrong with Rose and Crown. From classic UK fish and chips to more high end offerings, the menu is always a favorite of guests. Since the location doubles as a pub, they offer a variety of beers that are often more difficult to find in the United States. The whole restaurant makes for a creative dining location, but one that may not be the best fit for children.

Ultimately, that is the downfall of the entire World Showcase. Unless your kids are interested in the Agent P Adventure, which allows them to interact with hidden objects around the showcase, there isn't much that is focused directly on kids. Surprisingly though, I say that with a little hesitation for a few reasons. The World Showcase is still a blast for kids, especially with character interactions and kidcot stops in each country (kidcot is a kids only experience where cast members stamp a small take-home craft at each country). However, if your child isn't the most adventurous eater, it can often be tough to pick restaurants they will really enjoy. Disney is great at accommodating all guests, but there is a certain point where they have to either try to be authentic to the country's true heritage or develop their own menu items.

Fortunately, there is also one more reason to head over to Rose and Crown if you fall into that category. If you can time your dining reservation right, you can request outdoor seating and have an excellent view of IllumiNations. When you show up for your reservation time, take a minute to request outdoor seating and if you're willing to wait a few minutes extra they can usually make it happen. Sometimes it will take longer than expected, but they will always accommodate your request if they are able to.

If you can't get a reservation at Rose and Crown, be sure to check out the Yorkshire County Fish Shop. It is right next door, but is a small counter service window with outdoor seating serving fish and chips as well. The prices here are a little more reasonable than Rose and Crown, but creates a completely different dining experience. If that's better or worse has to be up to you, but they are both wonderful dining locations!

As you can see, the United Kingdom has a lot to offer. While you're passing through be sure to look around in a few of the little shops. You never know when you might find a treasure to take home with you. Personally, I believe some of the best Walt Disney World souvenirs come from the World Showcase, and it's easy to see why. The merchandise is usually something that you won't be able to get anywhere else, and the items will always accompany some kind of great story that can take you back to the parks.

Fragrances are a great example. Every day, you get to smell something from the parks that will really take you back to a special time with family at Walt Disney World. Scent is one of the greatest triggers of the memory. When you leave the parks, you won't really want that same Disney t-shirt that every other guest buys. You'll want something that tells a story in more than one way. Don't get me wrong, everyone loves a Disney t-shirt, but one of my favorite tips is to find that one item that you'll remember when and where you found it. If you can tie it to a story, it will be something that you will treasure forever. For example, it's not just coincidence that the confectionary on Main Street has a distinct scent. Disney figured out the emotional trigger scents can create in our minds and uses it to their advantage by utilizing artificial scents. Why shouldn't you have that opportunity everyday with a fragrance or even just an item that will take you back to some of your memories from Walt Disney World?

If you do decide to look for a scent, at the United Kingdom there is one of the more exclusive options. Under a special deal with Buckingham Palace, one of the merchandise locations actually carries a scent that can only be bought at Epcot and in Buckingham Palace! While this is just what a cast member told me, I have never seen it before and will probably never see it again outside of Epcot. Just imagine, you will never smell like anyone else and on top of that, you have a story to remember your purchase with that you get to experience each and every day!

International Gateway- Although this isn't really a pavilion included in the World Showcase, it is something that most people overlook completely and never take advantage of. The International Gateway is basically Epcot's second entrance. What most people don't realize is that this entrance leads directly out to the Boardwalk Resort as well as a boat that travels to the Boardwalk, Yacht and Beach Club, Swan and Dolphin, and ultimately ends at Hollywood Studios. If you have an annual pass or a park hopper ticket, this is a wonderful and time saving service. You can leave the park, head to one of the other destinations and come back later. In the resort section I mentioned all the Boardwalk and Yacht and Beach Club have to offer, but the Swan and Dolphin also have many restaurants open to the public that are just as wonderful. However, the Swan and Dolphin are not owned or operated by Disney, so the level of theming isn't quite the same.

I'll give you an explanation for how this can be useful. Say, for example, Epcot is packed for some reason. All you have to do is once you get to the back of the park, jump on a boat, get away from the crowds for a while, relax on a hammock outside of the Yacht and Beach Club, or even take a ride on a surrey bike at the Boardwalk (unfortunately the bikes aren't free). Most guests really don't even think about the fact that a resort is never going to ask you to leave and they invite guests to their property whenever they want to show up. The only things they reserve exclusively to overnight guests are pools and resort rooms. Everything else is there for anybody to use and the average guests never take advantage of that. I have spent many nights looking around the Boardwalk shops and restaurants and they treat you just like a guest. To be completely honest, they would never know if you were a guest or not, nor would they care.

In addition to all that lies outside the park gate, inside the park, there is a little gift shop and package pickup area. The package pickup service is overlooked as well by a majority of new guests. Surprisingly, any item bought in the Disney parks, not just Epcot Center, can be sent to the front of the park for pickup at the end of the day, sent to your resort for free, and I believe they will even ship it home for you. With the exception of the shipping home option, the rest of the services are completely free. Why carry a heavy package around the park when it can be waiting for you later on your way out? The International Gateway is one of the locations to pick up those packages, mainly for the guests leaving through the back exit.

As for the gift shop that accompanies the package pickup area, it really isn't much to write home about. It has a few fun little items, but nothing too special. Lastly, you can pick up your Agent P World Showcase Adventure guide right outside of the store. The adventure is pretty fun for kids, but not too incredibly elaborate. As you tour the countries, there are various places that interact with the guests partaking in the adventure. The experience is at your own pace and helps you really discover all of the little areas that aren't front and center in the various pavilions of the World Showcase. If you have never done it before, I would say to try it if you have kids, but to skip it completely if you don't. You won't be missing too much.

France- When you first see France, it looks incredibly small. No matter how funny that sounds, when referring to the pavilion it really is true. From a distance, France looks like a fancy little restaurant on the corner with a few fountains near by. For years I took a look at the stuff up front then walked right past without ever taking the time to explore a little farther into the pavilion. It was a huge mistake. When you take the time to actually travel back into the pavilion, it really seems to expand.The entire space actually has more to experience than about any other pavilion. I will warn you though, you may want to hide your wallet, because it's home to some of the most pricey shopping and dining in Epcot Center.

First off, you have Chefs de France on the corner. While this is one of two table service options available in France, it is definitely the more budget conscious. The food is French, as the pavilion implies, but the offerings aren't too elaborate to enjoy. Some of the more sought after items which are available include steak, soups, and even a few wonderful, traditional, French desserts. The setting is quite elegant and you can even choose to dine outside on the patio area if you so desire. As with the outdoor seating in the United Kingdom, here you can watch Illuminations from your table as well, but you'll have to time your reservation just right to view the show.

The other table service option is one that is on my list of what you must do at some point on a Disney vacation. It is called Monsieur Paul and is possibly one of the best dining experiences you can reserve at Walt Disney World. Short of dining at the incredibly luxurious Victoria and Albert's at the Grand Floridian, you will not find a better meal on the Disney property. The location itself is sort of out of the way, but is a "hidden secret" of Epcot as a result. Although the price is a bit much, the experience is well worth the cost and since the food focuses on more high end offerings, such as duck and seafood, the cost is somewhat understandable. Additionally, they offer some of the most delicious desserts in all of the World Showcase.

As with all of the best Disney experiences, the restaurant has a history that goes beyond the location itself. Monsieur Paul is backed by chef Bocuse of France. That world famous chef, known for his work at Auberge du Pont de Colognes, opened this location in addition to Chefs de France as his first restaurants in the

United States. Chefs de France was actually the first Bocuse backed restaurant and, more recently, Monsieur Paul became the second. As you can imagine from such a well known chef, the food at both locations is absolutely incredible. A second aspect, if that isn't enough to make you book already, is that many tables at Monsieur Paul have the best, unobstructed view of the World Showcase. It really is wonderful to see the showcase from above, but the views and wonderful food do come at a cost. For those on the dining plan, that cost is 2 table service dining credits, but if you pay out of pocket, prepare to be staggered by your bill.

If those two dining experiences aren't enough to make you want to spend a little more time in France, there is actually still a lot more to cover. As you can imagine, you can't have a France pavilion without a French bakery, and Disney didn't let us down with Les Halles Boulangerie and Patisserie. Now I can't tell you what that means, but what I can tell you is that this is one of the best bakeries I have ever been to. They have virtually one of every French dessert you can imagine and none of them are disappointing! From the chocolate mousse to the creme puffs and sandwiches, you really can't order anything that won't satisfy and exceed expectations.

Originally, the bakery was very small and hard to find. Recently it was relocated and is actually even harder to find, but it is much larger due to it's growing popularity. Don't expect a huge seating area or anything, but for a counter service option and snack location, you can only expect so much. Although today there is much more seating than in the past, there still isn't quite enough to accommodate everyone. Luckily, virtually everything they serve can be picked up and taken with you. The old location of the bakery has actually been transformed into another dessert option in the form of L'Artisan des Glaces, a small ice-cream shop. Personally, I have never tried the ice-cream, but how can you go wrong with dessert at Disney! As I mentioned above, the locations are a little hard to find, but just keep going back and you'll run into them near the back close to the exit of Impressions de France.

In addition to food, the France pavilion has a few featured shopping locations and even a film named Impressions de France. I always prefer the food, but the shopping isn't bad either. The merchandise locations offer a few unique fragrance and makeup offerings that are sometimes very difficult to find in the United States. A few of the more well known names in the fragrance world here are Guerlain and Givenchy. With both of these French brands being represented as well as many others, it makes for a great opportunity to have an exclusive fragrance buying experience. In regards to Geurlain in particular, the fragrance brand actually has its own signature store and embodies everything the Geurlain experience has to offer.

As you can imagine in France, they couldn't forget the wine. Other than in the restaurants, which have a decent selection, there is actually a location where you can taste and purchase various French wines. Although they would most likely have to be shipped home if you are flying, it is a great, authentic touch that really rounds out the French experience. To wrap up this pavilion, take a minute, if you have the time, to watch Impressions de France. It isn't a must do if you're short on time, but it gives a glimpse into what France is all about. Some enjoy it, some don't, but I'll leave that decision up to you.

Morocco- I'll be completely honest about Morocco. I don't really mind the design of the pavilion, but I really can't stand the smells and food that the area offers. Morocco has a very diverse culture, but Disney chose to use some of the more elaborate aspects that most Americans won't quite understand or enjoy. As with anything, some people will really like it, but it will never be on my Disney must do list. No matter how I feel about the pavilion, it is still part of Epcot Center and a location that you should definitely try for yourself. It never hurts to try everything once, but you're not going to enjoy everything about Walt Disney World, and that's part of the fun. You get to explore and discover new things every time you visit, and that's definitely a big part of the overall Disney experience. You're not going to enjoy it all, but everyone will find something to enjoy! That's the beauty of Disney.

The pavilion offers three Moroccan dining experiences with some quite exotic flavors. The first and most talked about is Spice Road Table which features a menu focusing on small plates and various drinks that all have a mediterranean influence. As for the physical location, it offers some great views, but also a unique themed dining room that really makes the experience. The second option is the only counter service location of the three restaurants in the pavilion. Tangierine Café, as it is called, is one of the most adventurous counter service locations on property. The food here isn't for the picky eater in any way, shape, or form. Also, due to the food they serve, it is one of the more expensive counter service locations as well. Lastly, we have Restaurant Marrakesh. The restaurant is elaborately Moroccan in theming, but does so in a sort of upscale way. Personally, the theming makes me a little uncomfortable, not because of the food or anything like that, but rather because it gives me a feeling of being in an Indiana Jones movie for some reason or another. The food is largely beef, lamb, and chicken dishes, but in addition, there is actually a show that goes on within the restaurant that features live belly dancers. Even though this is pretty creative on Disney's part, it isn't quite the best fit for a majority of families.

The rest of the pavilion is a kind of small Moroccan marketplace setup. You can buy rugs and little golden lamps that look like they came straight out of Aladdin. I don't believe that is the best representation of the country on Disney's part, but it could be. I'm definitely not an expert on Moroccan culture. So, in my opinion, this definitely isn't a place where I would say to spend a lot of time on your trip, but some guests could potentially enjoy it in one way or another.

Now I know that all of these comments seem a little negative toward the authenticity and representation of the country. However, if I focused on that aspect alone, I would be missing my own point in writing the book. There is always something beyond the surface with Disney and finding what that is is just another part of the Disney adventure. In this case, I had to look beyond the pavilion itself to realize why none of the disappointments I have with Morocco should have even mattered in the first place! The World Showcase isn't about representing the countries perfectly, it's about something much bigger that takes so many people so long to figure out.

For me, it took seeing Illuminations once again. I've seen the show many times, but with a different outlook, I understood what I had been missing. The showcase isn't about the countries, it's about the people. The whole goal is to show that cultures are different, but that we're all just people living slightly different lives. If anyone doesn't agree, just go watch Illuminations and it will all make sense. It has to be about bringing people together both in the world and within the park, and that's the part that I overlooked with Morocco. It doesn't matter if it's incredibly accurate, it's just meant to establish a goal and to create the overall idea the entire World Showcase is based upon. It's a good thing that it does portray that incredible message so well, because what many people don't know is that Illuminations is rumored to cost around $25,000 per show! Even if you don't include holiday costs, that means Illuminations costs Disney over 9 million dollars each year!

Japan- Following one of my least favorite pavilions is actually one of my favorite pavilions. Japan is a place that many of us will never have the opportunity to go visit, but Disney successfully brings many elements of the experience to Walt Disney World to give us a little piece of Japan in the heart of central Florida. There is so much to see in Japan that it's hard to find a good place to start. You can never go wrong with food, so why not start there?

The food in Japan appeals to a couple audiences, but can accommodate a variety of preferences. First, Tokyo Dining is a guest favorite. The food is great and has a variety of options including sushi, something called a bento box, and even a few more uniquely Japanese offerings straight from the grill. The draw here surprisingly isn't always the food, but rather the location. Its location is on the second floor of the large store in Japan giving you an unobstructed view of the World Showcase as well as a sushi bar. From what I can tell, this is the most popular of the four dining locations in Japan.

The second location is called Teppan Edo. Teppan Edo is right next to Tokyo Dining, but the menu is very different. The restaurant is a hibachi style experience. Each guest sits around a grill, and the food is prepared right in front of you in the form of a little show performed by Japanese Chefs. I would really recommend this for anyone looking for more than just food, but rather a destination. The meal can be quite time consuming, as with most hibachi, but it is well worth the wait.

The last real restaurant we have is Katsura Grill. The grill is a quaint little counter service location that offers bowls that include meat or fish. They also offer sushi at a semi-reasonable price point. Surprisingly, even though it is small, it is decently themed for a counter service location and has quite a few seats available to accommodate guests. Outside, there are also a few tables surrounding a garden with a fountain that is a quite relaxing place to sit and eat. Surprisingly, there is actually one more place to get food in Japan called Kabuki Cafe. I say "place to get food" for a reason. Kabuki Cafe is basically a little shack out by the main walkway where you can get a couple sushi items and a few drinks. The cafe really doesn't offer much, so if you really want to eat in Japan, take a few steps farther into the pavilion and get something a little better for about the same price at Katsura.

Other than dining, Japan has one of the best gift shops in all of the showcase, Mitsukoshi. If you enter the store from the front corner it seems to just keep going on forever. Every time you leave one room, another starts and you never think you'll find the end. There are so many unique items to purchase or view in the store that you could easily spend an hour in it and never see everything. One of the crown jewels of the store is the pick a pearl experience. If you choose, you can buy a clam and they will crack it open and give you the pearl inside. The pearls range in size and the whole experience comes with a personalized show special to each guest. Once you get your pearl, they will actually give you the opportunity to make it into a necklace or ring of your choice. The experience is great and the pearl can be used as a great gift, or a souvenir that accompanies a wonderful story. Another neat aspect of Mitsukoshi is the Sake bar in the very back of the store. Here, you can taste and even take home with you many different types of Japanese Sake which is an art form in Japanese culture. In this short paragraph, we have just touched on all that is available at Mitsukoshi, but there is so much available that we could write about it all day.

Through just these few parts of the Japan pavilion, you can see why it is one of the favorite pavilions of many guests, including myself. As a sort of honorable mention, take a minute to look up Candy Miyuki. As a part of the Japan pavilion for many years, there was a short show that demonstrated an almost lost art of molding candy at high temperatures by hand. Today, the show no longer exists, but the videos of Candy Miyuki's work are very easy to find and extremely entertaining to watch. After seeing it in person for so many years, it's quite strange to realize that it will likely never return.

The American Adventure- A lot of guests pass this pavilion and laugh for good reason. They can't help but think, "I'm in America, I'm pretty sure I know what it's like." I can't really blame them for that assumption, but the America pavilion actually focuses on American history rather than the current state of our nation. The pavilion itself actually has an attraction or, rather a show, that features the exact same name. Sometimes this confuses guests, but once you experience the show, the name choice makes a little more sense. Although it isn't the most creative title on Disney's part, the attraction really is worth seeing. The show itself is basically a movie that has the addition of Disney's iconic audio-animatronics. It follows the story of America's past and slowly moves into what the future could hold for the nation. Sadly, just like many of the other film based attractions across the World Showcase, it isn't the most interesting experience. The animatronics are pretty neat, but the show only appeals to a certain crowd. Usually, it is the same crowd that really enjoys the Hall of Presidents at Magic Kingdom.

The American Adventure is also home to some of the much more common food options. At a counter service location called Liberty Inn, you can order chicken, burgers, hotdogs, and about anything else that is iconically American cuisine. Liberty Inn is a great option for any type of picky eater, but to be honest, that would be the only scenario where I would recommend eating here. The food is kind of in the same ballpark as Electric Umbrella that we talked about earlier, but just like that location, there are far better dining options around the World Showcase. At least with the Electric Umbrella, it offers you an entertaining environment to a certain extent. At Liberty Inn, the entire dining area is simply a large seating area of all white tables and chairs. I can't really recommend this dining location, because there isn't much about it that creates a unique experience.

On the other hand, there is a little walk up location called Fife and Drum Tavern that is a great place to stop by just steps from the showcase walkway. The offerings here are extremely limited, but iconically Disney. The main item at Fife and Drum is the classic giant Disney turkey leg, despite popular belief that you can only get the turkey legs in the Magic Kingdom. Additionally, at the same location, there are a few frozen drink offerings and even beer on tap for those incredibly hot days that dominate the Florida weather patterns.

Sadly, unless you're feeling patriotic or it's one of the various festival times at Epcot while you are visiting the park, I wouldn't really bother spending much time at the American Adventure. Disney Imagineering really dropped the ball here. They could have done so much to make this area of the park great and to set the pace for the rest of the pavilions, but ultimately they did the exact opposite. With the exception of the International Gateway, which isn't even a pavilion, the American Adventure has less to offer than any other country represented in all of the showcase.

Italy- The Italy pavilion, similar to the France pavilion, is one that doesn't look very big from the outside, but opens up once you get farther back into it. From the replica fountains to the incredibly detailed architecture, Italy recreates the look and feel of the country itself in incredible detail. As always for me, the food is the best part. Even though it is the main table service location of the pavilion, Via Napoli Ristorante is one dining choice I overlooked for years and definitely regret. The pizza here is second to none, but has a unique flavor. However, the restaurant features various pastas as well.

The overall theming of Via Napoli is classy, but not off-putting in any way which allows it to be inviting for families as well as any other type of guest. One of the newest additions to the restaurant is a walk up pizza window. Although this separate area only sells pizza, you don't have to make a reservation to get a slice. That being said, and due to the fact that it is just a window, it only has bottled drinks, which is a little out of the ordinary for Disney parks. No matter which experience you choose, you really can't go wrong with this truly Italian experience.

If you are looking for a little more adult exclusive dining option, take a few steps next door to Tutto Gusto Wine Cellar. Although children are allowed to eat here, they aren't apart of the crowd most of the time. In most cases, the location is used as a wine tasting experience with offerings of both red and white wines. In addition to the drink tastings, there is also cheese, but more importantly, there is a limited menu. Although the offerings aren't the main focus, it is a great place to relax and get away from crowds and younger children for a little while. Kids are an integral piece of the Disney experience, but it's always nice to have a place to retreat for a little while within the parks.

Lastly, we have Tutto Italia. Although still distinctly Italian, Tutto Italia really encompasses that classic Italian look and feel. The food isn't much that most people rave about, but it appeals to a distinct crowd. Nearly every aspect of the restaurant screams upscale, but personally I prefer the atmosphere and menu of Via Napoli. However nice the restaurant is, the specialty title doesn't seem to fit in the same way it does for a location like Le Cellier. The experience doesn't seem to live up to the expectations many have for the location. That being said, that is really the only flaw I can find within the entire pavilion and, to be honest, it's a flaw I can live with. It's hard to fault Disney for having too high of standards at their dining locations. As a guest myself, I can't expect them to always beat the benchmark that they set in the first place with one of their other restaurants.

Once the dining is taken care of, take a look around, because you never know what kind of souvenir you'll find in Italy. They have a little bit of everything. You have the classic Italian brands in every store and even a few items that are unique to Epcot Center. In a similar way, be sure to search for and attempt to appreciate all the authentic details. To most, that's what sets Italy part. It's really hard to nail down one aspect of the decor that does it, but the area just seems to feel authentic in a way that not all the countries of the World Showcase do. Disney Imagineering went above and beyond once again and it is surprisingly obvious in the best possible way!

Germany- Germany is a country that very few people know much about in the real world. Epcot Center takes that knowledge and uses it for the guests benefit. You can enter the area and leave understanding something completely new. Surprisingly, it's a great feeling and one that so many guests don't expect to have in a theme park.

Now I'm not saying you'll learn the entire history of Germany by walking through the pavilion, because that's not really a realistic expectation. It's mostly a lot of little details that help build knowledge of a much larger country through very subtle applications. For instance, did you know the Werther's Candy Company is actually German? Disney creatively informs you of this while doing one of my favorite things! (As you can imagine at this point in the book, I'm referring to eating.) Within the pavilion, look for a shop called Karamell-Küche. The building is easy to miss, but hard to forget. On the inside, the smell is a bit overwhelming. The entire atmosphere takes on the aroma of melting caramel and popcorn which is incredibly hard not to enjoy. Despite a lot of other wonderful caramel based desserts that are offered here, the draw to the location has always been the caramel popcorn. If you haven't tasted hot and fresh caramel popcorn, you don't know what you're missing! If you try it for the first time here, you definitely won't think of popcorn the same way ever again!

Also included in Germany are a few of the more original shops of the World Showcase. At one location, there are various pewter figures that are incredibly intricate and hard to pass up, and at another elaborate steins are sold. The steins are something that can be used as decoration easily and really give you a story to tell when you get home. For me, thats the best kind of souvenir.

Beyond the stores, the food can be an experience as well. Biergarten, the table service location of the area features a buffet that is sure to serve at least one item that everyone in your party will enjoy. Although it isn't one of the most popular dining locations, it is definitely one of the more elaborate. When you enter the restaurant it's like entering a little German town. At the center of the dining room, there is a small stage that hosts live entertainment in celebration of Octoberfest. At Biergarten, it's Octoberfest every single day! Even though the theming isn't for everyone, Disney really nailed the German influence in both the food and the elaborate entertainment.

The other location, Sommerfest, is much simpler and has an extremely limited menu. Basically, all the menu has to offer is bratwurst, potato salad, and beer. Although that's not really a bad thing, it does limit who will have a desire to eat here. It is a counter service location, as you can imagine, but the limited offerings make it hard to recommend. However, between Karamell-Küche, Biergarten, and Sommerfest, its hard not to find something fun to do in Germany, despite its lack of a true "attraction".

China- As we get into the final three pavilions, it's hard to think it can get much better than what has already been mentioned. Surprisingly, when you start at Canada, you end up saving the best three countries for last. China definitely doesn't disappoint, and the pavilion is incredibly immersive. As you approach the area, you are greeted with a cultural representation that you may or may not have ever seen before, juggling sticks. While at first they seem a little intimidating, you are invited to try them for yourself and with the guidance of friendly cast members, anyone can learn how it's done. If you end up really enjoying it, you can even pick out a set to take home with you for a fairly reasonable price. The juggling sticks have become an icon of the World Showcase and are definitely one of the more sought after souvenirs.

Once you get farther into China, it really starts to come alive. The koi ponds lead the way to a show called Reflections of China, and the film itself is in circle vision 360. Although it isn't the most interesting attraction, it provides guests with a deeper look into the history and society of the country. As weird as it may sound, the way they film the circle vision experiences is actually quite a bit more interesting than the actual films. To create an image that surrounds the audience on all sides, a special camera is used to film a scene for the 360 degree viewing area. The camera is actually a combination of multiple cameras filming in many different directions. The incredibly high tech design is then mounted to a helicopter which slowly hovers over various places used in the creation of the films. The most amazing aspect is that these films were not made in the age of our modern technology, but rather over 30 years ago!

As with each of the other pavilions, China has its own food locations. Chinese food isn't all that foreign to most American people, but the dining locations in the China pavilion actually go beyond americanized Chinese food and dive a little deeper into the cultural food items. Nine Dragons, the only table service location, is a great example of the more authentic Chinese offerings. The menu features a variety of classic Chinese dishes, but also some of the more creative as well. For those looking for a more distinct and adventurous dining experience, Nine Dragons is probably a great option. It does offer many more mainstream menu items as well, so it can really appeal to a variety of guests. The restaurant is not the most popular from my booking experience, but that usually just means it is often overlooked. If for some reason you do need a last minute dining reservation, this is the place to go. There is normally walk up reservations readily available, so always at least try to investigate this option before settling for a counter service offering, especially if you are on the dining plan.

At Disney, there aren't many bad dining experiences, just some that are better than others. You can't really go wrong, and I can almost guarantee you will at the very least leave content, but most likely impressed with any restaurant on property. An additional dining location comes in the form of the Lotus Blossom Cafe. Lotus Blossom is a counter service offering for the less adventurous eaters. I really like the location, but it doesn't offer a lot more then your local Chinese take-out would. However, the quality of the food is much better than a Chinese take-out restaurant.

The atmosphere in the China pavilion is incredibly relaxing. If you had the time, you could probably walk around the place for hours. There is just so much to take in. The view of the lake is incredible and the koi pond within the pavilion is quite beautiful as well. In addition to the views, there is a unique balancing show that is definitely worth waiting for. Once the show begins, you will be amazed at the talent of the performers. There are no tricks, no stage, just a small section of concrete and incredible skill on display. As you can clearly see, there is quite a bit to see and do in the China area, but that can be said about the entire World Showcase. So, at this point, I can't help but recommend that if you want to experience most of what the World Showcase has to offer, you may have to take more than one day to explore everything that sparks your interest.

Norway- In the past, Norway was undoubtedly my favorite pavilion. Notice how I say in the past. As with many guests, I am starting to lose interest in it for one main reason that has been debated for many months amongst the Disney community. Recently, Walt Disney Imagineering announced that the original Maelstrom attraction will be replaced by a Frozen themed attraction. Not surprisingly, that sparked an enormous amount of controversy as to whether or not the movies belong in the showcase. No matter what we as the guests think, Disney is proceeding with the construction and pretty soon, we will have a new attraction featuring the same track, but with a much different story. Personally, I can understand the decision from a business standpoint, but from a nostalgia standpoint, it is hard to come to grips with. However, the Disney parks weren't created for nostalgia, but rather for innovation in the first place.

The Norway pavilion is still wonderful to visit, but it seems to be a little less representative of the country itself with the new additions. Surprisingly, there are only three main draws to the pavilion during the construction, but it is still one of the more creative sections of the showcase. The first and biggest draw has to be the Princess Storybook Dining at Akershus Royal Banquet. As the only character meal in the World Showcase, Akershus is a table service reservation that is fairly hard to come by. Even though the food isn't the best, the character experience usually makes up for it. The characters at the restaurant are exclusively princesses, as it's name implies, but if you want that Cinderella's Royal Table experience for a much lower price point, this has to be your go to restaurant choice. The character interaction is nearly identical and it is significantly easier to obtain a reservation for Akershus. Even though Disney claims the food to be Norwegian, it's largely American and appeals to virtually any age guest. As a step down to a counter service location, Kringla Bakeri Og Kafe offers many wonderful pastries and even a few sandwiches. As a similar option to that of the bakery in France, Kringla isn't quite as extensive in pastry offerings, but the ones they do offer are definitely enjoyable.

One of the more interesting features of the Norway pavilion is the little store next to the bakery. Even though the merchandise features trolls and viking helmets, there is also a subtle nod to modern culture in the way of a fragrance. Geir Ness' line of products are sold in this merchandise location and add a wonderful sensory experience to the store. Despite what you may expect, the scents themselves are priced fairly reasonably, but the fragrance's story is much more unique than the item itself. When Geir Ness designed this iconic scent, he became the only

Norwegian fragrance creator. He set a goal and came to America to distribute the product and that's how it ended up in Epcot Center. Today, the fragrance greets guests in the store each and every day. The scents, given that there is a cologne as well as a perfume and other products, really take you back to the Norway Pavilion at Epcot. Over time, it has become iconic for many Disney parks enthusiasts and may just become your next go to fragrance.

Mexico- I like to think we've saved the best for last. The Mexico pavilion offers just about anything you can imagine. There is plenty of shopping, dining, entertainment, and even a boat ride with The Three Caballeros. The pavilion itself has never been abandoned in a way some of the others seem to have been. Disney Imagineering is always making efforts to keep the pavilion new and fresh by making subtle changes that make a big difference over time. The largest of the recent additions came in the way of La Cantina de San Angel. San Angel is one of the best counter service options of the entire World Showcase. The food is authentic, but not too adventurous for anyone to enjoy. The nachos really steal the show, and they are definitely a guest favorite. However, the atmosphere is also great, which is something you don't always find at counter service locations. The seating is mostly outdoors, but there is quite a bit of it. Also, with its location on the waterfront, the views are always great, especially at night.

The best part of the seating is the part that most people overlook; the interior seating at lunch and occasionally at dinner as well. If you go toward the area that sits out on the water, look over to your left and there will be two big doors that are almost always closed. If you open the doors, you can enter a large seating area that is used during the day for San Angel and at night for La Hacienda de San Angel. La Hacienda is actually a table service location, but a portion of the dining room is open to La Cantina guests most of the time. As a result, the seating is quite nice and the views out the window at the World Showcase lake are great, especially with the comforts of air conditioning. Virtually no guests take advantage of this seating area, so it is very easy to find a seat and a great place to enjoy a meal.

Now this is where the dining locations in Mexico get a little confusing. You have three main locations that all have San Angel in the title. This can be extremely confusing when making reservations, but hopefully this will make it a little easier to keep them separate. La Cantina we already covered, but La Hacienda has only been mentioned. The location has the same great views as the shared seating area with La Cantina, but is a completely different dining experience. The food is much more authentic than just tacos, quesadillas, and nachos. La Hacienda fills the profile of a more cultural dining offering and features much more creative menu items that aren't found at all Mexican-American style restaurants across the United

States. Additionally, inside of the pavilion, there is the San Angel Inn. As another table service location, the Inn fills the gap between the more adventurous La Hacienda and the relatively simple La Cantina. The Inn has a little something for everyone, but unfortunately, it doesn't always get the best reviews from guests. That being said, the atmosphere can make up for the sub-par food. The seating area is just beyond the marketplace that covers a majority of the pavilions interior and borders the waters edge of the Gran Fiesta Tour. The room itself is one of the most immersive on the Disney property and creates an experience that can only be had at Walt Disney World and in Mexico itself.

Lastly, we have one more creative location that can be considered dining, but is more of a bar than an actual dining option. La Cava del Tequila is a place that many of the Disney passholders love. Basically, it's a Tequila Bar, but one with an enormous amount of options. Additionally, it's a good place to hang out for a while in a lounge style atmosphere that is very inviting. There is a short list of appetizers to order from as well, but they aren't really the focus of the experience and, as a result, La Cava del Tequila is not a part of the Disney Dining Plan.

In a section of the park that isn't known for the attractions, the Gran Fiesta Tour Starring The Three Caballeros fills a void in a great way. The attraction has evolved over the years and even quite recently, but the experience has always been one that people of all ages can enjoy. Don't expect an Imagineering marvel, but it is a great way to spend a few minutes and round out a trip through the Mexico pavilion. Surprisingly, one of the most recent additions to Epcot Center is actually found in the Gran Fiesta Tour. Although it isn't a major change, it will appeal to those who appreciate the history behind the attractions. The addition came in the form of the long awaited return of the Three Caballeros animatronics back to Walt Disney World. For those of you who don't know, the animatronics were originally a part of the Mickey Mouse Revue at Magic Kingdom until it closed. Then, they were sent oversees to be used in another attraction. They have been gone for many years, and it is great that they have finally returned "home" to Walt Disney World. It really enhanced the casual boat ride and added a little surprise for the Disney enthusiasts.

As you can see, Epcot offers just about anything you could want out of a theme park. It has the rides that take your breath away, but it also sets the stage for an adventure of a lifetime. There is no other place in the world that lets you experience so many countries in such a simple way. The experience is hard to put into words, but you won't want to miss the opportunity to visit. So many guests look at the park map online or when they enter the park and see that there aren't that many attractions. Then, they get a disappointed look on their face and assume that they'll only be there for part of the day. That assumption couldn't be farther from the truth.

The Epcot experience doesn't come from the attractions alone, but rather the details of the experience, and it doesn't get much more detailed than the World Showcase. You don't want to go to the parks for the attractions anyway. If you do, I hate to be the bearer of bad news, but the Disney parks probably aren't for you. Although there are some incredible attractions, the attractions themselves aren't what make most vacations memorable. When you go in with this attraction focused plan of attack, you can't help but have a stressful, lackluster, and overall disappointing experience. As I have said many times, it is impossible to see and do everything. I've been in the Disney parks for years, and there are still several things I am happy to admit I have never had the opportunity to experience. If you haven't already noticed, I use the word experience quite often, but it's for a purpose. An experience is something you remember forever, where as a ride or simply a restaurant doesn't alway have that same affect on its own.

Disney does an incredible job of merging those two concepts in Epcot Center. The restaurants and attractions are great, but the experience is what keeps the guests coming back. That idea was the entire goal of the original Epcot Center design. It was something that was going to revolutionize modern society and create a great leap forward in innovation. Unfortunately, that lofty goal never really played out in the way it was intended to, but the rendition of Epcot we have today still holds on to that original goal of merging experience with culture in a way that all too often gets overlooked. It's hard for me to believe that a park with over 30 dining options will never be complete, but that's one of the many joys of Epcot. It's always growing and changing in ways that are so hard to put into words, but that will continue to create memories that will last a lifetime.

DISNEY'S HOLLYWOOD STUDIOS

Hollywood Studios has evolved over the years, but has always been a park that Disney has never quite figured out a theme for. In it's early days as a working studio for productions such as the Mickey Mouse Club, Hollywood Studios played a role in the lives of kids across the nation. Today it accomplishes that same goal, but in a completely different way. Unfortunately, Disney has decided to get away from the complications of managing a studio at the same time and place as an amusement park and has begun to focus on the concept of putting guests into the movies instead. To me, there isn't really anything wrong with that, but now there is a sort of mixed theming throughout the park.

On one hand, you have a behind the scenes look at making the movies we all know and love, but on the other hand you have attractions developing that are designed to immerse you in the stories of the films. Although the ideas are similar, they also seem a little contradictory, which has led to a misguided park. Thankfully, with the recently announced expansions with Star Wars and Toy Story the studios seem to be getting a more guided theme, but that may also take away from the parks' roots. Either way, I am sure it will be for the better, because both themes have an enormous amount of potential.

The overall experience at Hollywood Studios is much more quaint than the other Disney parks and it makes for a wonderful experience. With a new direction and a new focus, we can only assume that big things are to come in the near future. A name change is rumored, two new lands are being built, and who knows what else Disney has in store? But, for now, we will just have to enjoy all that the park currently offers.

A lot of people claim the studios is a half day park, and some even say it's not even worth going to in its current state. The half day portion of that argument, I can understand if you're not looking to ride everything in the park. However, to skip the park completely would be a mistake. There are so many experiences in Hollywood Studios that give you that "Wow!" moment the very first time you partake in them that if you were to skip the park completely, you would really be missing out. To show you what I mean, we'll have to get into the many attractions the park offers and analyze what's here to stay and what's rumored to go.

HOLLYWOOD BOULEVARD: The real Hollywood Boulevard in California isn't much to look at, but here in Disney's Hollywood Studios, that is definitely not the case. From the moment you enter the park, the "main street" comes into view and is actually a rendition of Hollywood Boulevard. You can't miss the area and I'm not really sure why you would ever want to. Just like at the Magic Kingdom, plenty of shopping can be found here, but surprisingly, the gift shops have some Hollywood Studios exclusive merchandise. For instance, you can buy Aerosmith merchandise due to Rockin' Roller Coaster, but you can also purchase custom embroidered towels right next door. The merchandise is a great change from the repetitive items found at many of the other retail locations across property. Even though there is plenty of shopping to do on Hollywood Boulevard, it's not until you get to the very end of the street that you find an actual attraction.

The Great Movie Ride- The Great Movie Ride is the one attraction on Hollywood Boulevard and it doesn't disappoint. Originally, The Great Movie Ride was essentially covered up by the Sorcerer's hat that had become Hollywood Studio's icon after it overstayed it's original, intended, time on display. Recently, Disney realized the issue and actually removed the Sorcerer's hat completely. Now, just as when the park originally opened, The Great Movie Ride has become the icon once again.

With that being said, the outside of the attraction is quite spectacular, being that it is an almost exact replica of the real Chinese Theatre. There is actually a rumor that Disney was involved with a law suit over the design and legal rights to the architecture. The past ownership, who had rights to the buildings design, did not want to give Disney permission to use their design for the attraction. Eventually, Disney made a compromise and avoided legalities by agreeing to find a way that the entire facade of the attraction could never be seen all at once. By creating the Sorcerers Hat, they did just that. Recently, Turner Classic Movies made a partnership with the Chinese Theatre and, coincidentally, Disney partnered with Turner Classic Movies for a partial redesign of The Great Movie Ride. It could be a coincidence, as I've mentioned, but it's hard to believe that a deal for classic movies to be shown once again in the Chinese Theatre could just happen to coincide with the hat being removed. It almost had to be a part of the TCM deal with Disney, as well as the owners of the theater's design rights.

As for the actual attraction, it features a slow moving guided journey into classic films such as the Wizard of OZ, Fantasia, Casablanca, and many more. The kicker on this attraction is that you have a live tour guide that makes the movies come alive, quite literally! From the youngest of guests to the oldest, it's hard to find someone that doesn't enjoy this attraction. You never have the same experience twice and it always has a way of immersing you in classic Hollywood the way it was supposed to be. Unfortunately, I do have to give one word of warning. There is one scene that is taken out of Alien that could frighten a few small children. It is a very short part of the experience, but definitely something you may want to look out for.

The Trolley Car Café- As a part of the addition of Starbucks to every Disney theme park, the Trolley Car Café fills that role in Hollywood Studios. Originally, the space for this dining location was used for a small gift shop, but the merchandise items that were sold here are now sold in the other numerous shopping location throughout the park. The design and theming of the café is pretty clever, and it really does make you feel as if you are in a trolley station.

Although the theming is wonderful, you don't really get much time to enjoy it. There is no place to sit down and it basically turns into a grab and go style counter service location. The food is pretty limited as well. Of course the main draw is the Starbucks coffee, but beyond the drinks, the menu is very limited to a few breakfast style sandwiches and bakery items. The pastries are great, just like at any other Disney bakery, but there really is nothing too special to say about the food, no matter how clever the design of The Trolley Car Café may be.

The Hollywood Brown Derby- Where the Trolley Car Café lacks special food, this location is the definition of it. Brown Derby is a classic Hollywood restaurant with theming everyone expects from the booming theatre era. From the classy atmosphere, to the high quality food, you really can't go wrong with this table service location. Surprisingly, the location isn't too hard to get a reservation for, but it does require two table service credits on the standard Disney Dining Plan. Also, the quality of the food comes at a significant price point. There are much more expensive dining locations across Walt Disney World, but the Brown Derby is definitely on the pricier end of the scale. To give merit to the claim of a quality atmosphere, Disney offers an experience to dine with an Imagineer with a certain fee. Nearly every time you book that experience, the meal is held at the Brown Derby. If Disney sends their own Imagineers there to eat, the food has to be some of the best the company offers.

The menu itself has a variety of options, but the majority consists of steak and seafood, and slightly cheaper options in the way of pasta and chicken are also available. The dining experience itself actually has a unique history. Hollywood Brown Derby used to be a part of a restaurant chain that was based out of California. Disney brought the restaurant in as a way of actually bringing California to central Florida in the most authentic way possible. Today, the restaurant chain has virtually disappeared with the exception of the one in

Hollywood Studios. The experience is as true to California as you can get and really makes for a wonderful dining experience.

ECHO LAKE: The Echo Lake section of the park is where the misguided nature of the theming starts to show itself. The lake itself isn't really a lake, but rather a small pond with a gigantic fake dinosaur in the middle of it. It just doesn't make sense. At one end, you have the adventure focused area of the park with Star Wars and Indiana Jones, but at the other end it holds on to the classic Hollywood feel. Recently, speculation has developed that this is where the Star Wars Expansion will begin as a result of the misguided theming in the area. Although that hasn't been confirmed by Disney, it is the place that would make the most sense. Star Tours is along the back side of Echo Lake and we already know that the streets of America are going away. Facing that reality, the area may change drastically in the upcoming years, but here are the attractions that are available for the time being.

Star Tours- The Adventures Continue- For the Star Wars fan, Star Tours is the pinnacle of all attractions. As you can imagine, with the new movies hitting theaters and the franchise growing exponentially, the attraction is becoming significantly more popular. Additionally, and as a result of the new film, the attraction has developed into a much more randomized experience. The best way to describe it is that every time you ride, it will almost always be a different experience.

With the initial upgrade to the ride system a couple of years ago, which added The Adventure Continues to the title, the attraction went from having one main show to having a randomized selection that was picked out of almost 100 variations. Basically, they created an attraction with almost unlimited re-ride value. Even more recently, an additional show has been added to the extensive randomized line up. The new experience features the characters that were a part of The Force Awakens film which debuted around Christmas in 2015.

As you can imagine, the attraction will potentially have a series of updates as the new group of movies are released. If you didn't already know, the Disney company has actually acquired Lucasfilm in order to produce new movies in the series. Hopefully, Disney will make the best of this opportunity to grow the brand and, in part, the Star Tours attraction.

During the latest D23 expo in Anaheim California, Disney released plans that look as if they will implement the Star Wars brand into the parks in an incredible new way that began with the Star Tours overlay. Surprisingly, the new shows will just be the tip of the iceberg when it comes to the proposed expansion.

The new experiences have not been completely unveiled, but the expo did release the concepts for the future possibility of boarding the Millennium Falcon and even stepping foot into the Cantina.

In this new land, Disney claims you will have the ability to be fully immersed in a new galaxy never before seen in the movies, complete with realistic droids and other unique surprises. It sounds as if this will be the next step in defining the immersion that could become the potential goal for Hollywood Studios in the years to come. There has been no time frame listed for the expansion construction, but if recent Disney renovation time frames are any indication, it may be at least a few years before it starts to fully develop.

As for Star Tours itself, the attraction is very similar to a high end motion theatre. You enter a room that has the ability to tilt and oscillate in various directions corresponding to the film on screen. Although this doesn't sound extremely intense, I would caution anyone who gets motion sick not to partake in this attraction. Personally, it seems as if the enclosed design creates motion sickness in a way that is more intense than even Expedition Everest. The ride vehicle is basically the same as what used to be found in the Wonders of Life Pavilion at Epcot for the Body Wars attraction. Unfortunately, Body Wars no longer exists, but if you ever had the opportunity to ride it, you have a fairly decent comparison as to what the Star Tours attraction is like.

Once your journey through space ends, if you are a Star Wars enthusiast, be sure to look through Tatooine Traders. The location features almost exclusively Star Wars merchandise in an immersive atmosphere. Unfortunately, this is the only Star Wars exclusive shopping location on property, so if they don't have what you want at Tatooine Traders, you aren't likely to find it anywhere else at Walt Disney World.

Indiana Jones Epic Stunt Spectacular!- The stunt show, although a great show, may be coming to an end quite soon. With the announced Star Wars expansions, it is a common consensus that the show could be either moved or done away with completely within the next few years. That assumption has been fueled by the claimed expansiveness of the new land, but also by Disney's abandonment of new ideas for the show itself. I have personally seen the show hundreds of times, but it never seems to change. Occasionally, there will be a very slight added element to one of the scenes, but ultimately Disney has done absolutely nothing with the stunt show since it's debut.

With that reality on the table, I can't really say the show needs to change all that much. It serves it's purpose to inform the guests of how a stunt based production is developed in a humorous, and extremely entertaining way. The show can appeal to just about any audience, but it is extremely loud at a few particular moments due to explosives and simulated gunfire used in the production. The Indiana Jones incorporation is authentic, but as you can imagine, Harrison Ford is nowhere to be found. The scenes are similar to those found across the Indiana Jones series, but aren't quite the same, intentionally. Overall, it is very entertaining and actually quite popular, so be prepared to get there early to get a good seat or you could end up standing in the back rather than sitting. The stunt spectacular doesn't run constantly as most Disney attractions do, but there are a variety of shows spread throughout the day. Be sure to grab a time guide when you enter the park or at most of the merchandise locations to get the most up to date information on the times for each of the shows for your allotted day at Hollywood Studios.

Hollywood and Vine- As one of the few table service locations that is ultimately family focused, Hollywood and Vine leaves a lot to desire most of the time. Although it is a buffet style meal, there isn't much good to say about the food or the atmosphere other than that it is a character meal. The food isn't horrible, but it is definitely hard to recommend. In the past, the meal items were actually pretty good, but more recently the quality of the entire experience has been slipping.

The characters are currently from various Disney Junior shows at breakfast and lunch, but at dinner the characters are usually Minnie and friends or none at all. The character interaction is about on the same level as the food right now. Each time a character comes to your table, they seem rushed to get to the next table, which is the complete opposite of most of the character meals on property. Overall, the food is decent, but the experience as a whole is really hard to recommend at the character meal price point.

The bright side comes from the various special packages available throughout the year. One of the more constant options is the Fantasmic! Dinner Package. With the package, you actually get to dine then head on over to Fantasmic! for special designated seating and the ability to bypass the line that is usually very long. Although this is an opportunity only available on certain dates, it is definitely one to take advantage of whenever you can. There are other special dining offers as well, but they vary largely from year to year. Not surprisingly, these special dining offerings usually accompany an additional cost for the meal and to be completely honest, most aren't worth the price.

50's Prime Time Café- Prime Time is definitely a very strange restaurant and one you kind of have to prepare yourself for. Once you walk in the door, you realize something isn't normal, but it's supposed to be that way. The whole experience is based on the idea of walking into a 1950's household and all that accompanies that environment. The waiters may poke fun at you, complain about putting your elbows on the table, or even make you finish all of your vegetables. Always be sure to listen, because you never know when they might send you to time out for misbehaving. The whole design makes for a very entertaining experience, but be sure to pack a good sense of humor when you decide to dine at Prime Time Café. Everything they do is in good fun and it all undoubtedly makes for some great memories with friends and family.

The food follows suit with the rest of the theme. Everything tastes home-cooked, and the menu is exactly what you would find in most households in the 50's. There are all the "country-style" favorites on the menu, including fried chicken, meatloaf, pot roast, and just about anything else your grandmother would cook. As you can imagine, with a menu full of comfort food, it's pretty delicious if you can appreciate the atmosphere. It definitely isn't everyone's cup of tea, but can be a lot of fun if it fits your personality.

Tune-Inn Lounge- The lounge location is right next door to 50's Prime Time Café and fits a similar theme with the same menu upon request. However, the main draw to the location are the specialty cocktails and other alcoholic beverages. One of the most popular features a glow in the dark ice cube that you get to take home with you once your drink is finished. The atmosphere is classic, just like Prime Time with 50's TV shows playing and some 50's furniture spread around the room. Given that it is a bar, it's not always the most family-oriented location, but it's still a really entertaining experience.

Min and Bill's Dockside Diner- If you remember that boat I talked about earlier, that's basically all there is to this counter service location. There is no indoor seating, the outdoor seating is limited, and there are just a few food offerings. The menu has changed quite a bit over the years, but most recently, the location features specialty macaroni and cheese and a few other less permanent options. The menu seems to be changing fairly often, which makes it a little hard to recommend when there are so many other counter service locations close by. You never quite know what to expect on the menu when you walk up to order, and that's not really a good thing.

Oasis Canteen- Oasis Canteen is a similar design to Min and Bill's, but focuses mostly on dessert items. The counter service location is more of a snack cart than an actual building. It's actually a little shack outside of the Indiana Jones stunt show that fits with the theme of the show. All they really offer is soft serve ice cream and funnel cakes. Fortunately, you can't really go wrong with those offerings, so if you're looking for dessert, be sure to stop by and check out Oasis Canteen.

Backlot Express- The Backlot Express is the counter service location that I recommend the most in the Echo Lake area. The food offerings are far better than any of the other small, walk-up locations, and the Backlot Express has extensive seating options. As a part of the dining room design, there is a pretty elaborate level of theming. The location plays up the role of a prop storage area for big, on screen, films. Although, to my knowledge, the props weren't actually used in any of the movies Disney has made over the years, it definitely creates a fun atmosphere with a lot to look at while you eat. As I mentioned, there are quite a few items on the menu, but it's pretty much your standard fast food offerings. However, this counter service location is far better than all of the other Echo Lake food choices.

STREETS OF AMERICA: The Streets of America are quite possibly the most underestimated portion of Hollywood Studios. They are not home to any big thrill rides or any high-end dining experiences, but the streets do create an interesting setup. Basically, this section of the park is focused around a huge movie set facade of the various iconic streets across the country. Although none of the buildings are real, the illusion they create is quite life-like. The facades are almost identical to what is used in big Hollywood productions.

Sadly, I'm going to have to start saying the Streets of America were instead of the Streets of America are. As a part of the expansions coming to Hollywood Studios, the streets are being completely removed, along with virtually everything else nearby. As you can imagine, this is creating quite a bit of confusion and changes in this area of the park. Some things are staying, and some things are going away, but I'll list both below just to cover everything that could potentially end up staying.

Pizza Planet- I know by simply hearing that name, the little kid inside everyone reading this just got really excited. Every Disney fan, at some point or another, has always wanted to eat at Pizza Planet from Toy Story. Well, just beyond the Streets of America, you can have that iconic experience complete with pizza, video games, and even a few green aliens. Although the recreation is nothing like the one pictured in the original movie, the representation still sparks that feeling of nostalgia for that great Pixar film. Believe it or not, the original Toy Story movie debuted over 20 years ago in 1995. Somehow, this iconic film has stood the test of time and continues to bring joy to kids of all ages and, of course, the kids at heart even today.

I know I can't mention Pizza Planet without talking about the food. Although the location is counter service, the menu items are actually very good and a great change from the standard burgers and fries found at most counter service locations. The pizza comes in the form of personal pan pizzas with a few different topping offerings. Not surprisingly, the main options are pepperoni and cheese, but there are other choices as well. On the dining plan, you get a side salad or a bag of chips with your pizza, as well as a dessert and a drink.

No matter what your preference, the food is incredibly good and the atmosphere will not disappoint. The only complaint that ever comes from this restaurant is that it can be quite loud and the seating is usually fairly crowded. The first issue I can't really help you out with, but the second one has a fairly simple fix. The noise is a result of the games and the guests having a good time playing the games, which is completely understandable. However, the seating issue is a simple fix. When you get in line to order your food simply send a member of your group to grab a table. The trick to getting a spot is to avoid the first floor and outdoor seating. It really isn't the best seating setup and is incredibly hard to find an empty table on the first floor. If you go upstairs, there is significantly more seating and always more availability. Although both areas are nearly always crowded, by the time you get ordered, someone in your group will have found a seat.

The line for Pizza Planet can get quite long, but it really is worth the wait. If not for the food alone, wait for the experience. I have been here multiple times and, sometimes, multiple times within the same trip, and have never been disappointed. I know this is going to sound like a Disney marketing moment, but the place really just seems magical. You can be having a really rough day in the park and walk in to Pizza Planet, sit down for a while, and everything seems to get better. I'm not sure if it's the music from the movies, the air conditioning on a hot day, or just the food being a good change of pace, but something is definitely special about this place.

Personally, I can remember a day that wasn't too out of the ordinary for a Florida summer, where it had been miserably hot all day then the rain rolled in early in the afternoon. Shows started to shorten or cancel due to the weather and the whole day seemed to be falling apart. Then we took a break for lunch. Naturally, we went to our favorite counter service location, Pizza Planet. By the time we finished the meal, we didn't really care that it was raining or that we were missing shows or any of that. We were just happy to be there and finished off the day in a wonderful way. For some reason, that will be a memory I will have for a lifetime. I don't know if it was running through the rain, or having to just go with the flow and see what happened next, but it was a day that went from a disaster to a memory that I'll never forget.

All that happened that day was a change that can only be described as magical. Somehow, the Disney parks have a way of allowing guests to have an incredible experience even on the worst of days. You can trudge through the rain all day, but have a huge smile on your face the entire time. You see, memories aren't made by the attractions or dining experiences, but rather by the moments you spend with those you care the most about. Without exaggerating at all, I bet 90% of my memories from Walt Disney World have no connection to an attraction. The other 10% are only connected to the attractions because of the responses of the people on the attraction, not the physical ride itself.

If you add that up, I'm quite literally saying that an attraction has never been my desire to return to Walt Disney World. Some people may say I'm crazy, but at some point or another during your vacation, you'll have that eye opening moment where you really will understand. As I've said throughout the entire book, the attractions aren't what make the experience magical, but rather the people who you experience them with. Everyone has that moment where they finally get it. It may seem like it will never happen, but when you least expect it, your mind will be blown and you'll never forget that feeling. That's what keeps us coming back!

Muppet Vision 3D- Although it's hard to transition back to attractions after that little tangent, there's no better way to do so than with something as iconic as The Muppets. Most of you will remember The Muppets from their original tv series many years ago, but many of you may recognize them from the remake of their show that is on tv today. Either way, the characters have become icons in our culture, and Muppet Vision 3D is no different. Just like the tv series, Muppet Vision 3D is fun for all ages while featuring witty humor and slapstick comedy. The show includes all of your favorite characters, but also one new one. The 3D effects aren't perfect since the show has been around for quite some time, but it is still highly entertaining. Once you throw in some full size, in person characters and of course the penguin band, the experience is a must-do in Hollywood Studios. Surprisingly, the show hardly ever has a wait longer than 20 minutes and averages around a 5 to 10 minute wait time. At the Disney parks, you really can't beat that short of a wait!

Mama Melrose's Ristorante Italiano- Mama Melrose's is one of the better hidden secrets of Hollywood Studios. The restaurant isn't too flashy; there is no big sign out front, and to be honest, it is actually pretty difficult to find if you don't know where to look. The spot for the dining location itself is just past Pizza Planet and tucked away in a corner of the park. Not surprisingly, unless you make your reservations randomly, it's not likely that anyone will tell you to book this restaurant. I understand that sounds like a bad thing, but it really isn't. Most people just overlook Melrose's, because it's not as "in your face" as the other dining options throughout the Disney parks. The food is classic Italian, but a little more on the authentic side, rather than the americanized Italian we often get in the United States. All I'm saying by that is that some more picky eaters may not like the offerings found at this dining location.

As for the atmosphere, it is one of the simpler themes that can be found in the Disney parks, but ultimately stays true to its more Italian roots. The seating is simple and sort of feels like a local New York or Chicago style pizza place with a slightly elegant flare. Overall, it may not be your favorite table service experience on the Disney property, but you really can't go wrong with Italian food. Additionally, the prices aren't too high compared to other options in Hollywood Studios, but as with any Disney dining, it's far from cheap. With that being said, Mama Melrose's Ristorante Italiano is a great option if you're looking to have a sit down meal and a little time away from the crowds that seem to be constantly growing.

Lights, Motors, Action! Extreme Stunt Show- To my surprise, the stunt show got a lot of negative press, especially with local guests, and I haven't quite figured out why. In my opinion, the stunt show was one of the best shows in all of the Disney Parks. It appealed to families, teenagers, adults, and the list goes on and on. The only downside I could find for the attraction would be it's lack of repeat value. All that means is that it is often something that if you've seen it once, you may not be compelled to see it multiple times after that. For some guests, that could be the case, but for me, that couldn't be further from reality. The show was mesmerizing.

Unfortunately, all of that was in past tense for a reason. With the expansions coming to Hollywood Studios, the area will be used for Toy Story or Star Wars Land. Disney released that this attraction along with the playground and studio catering company will be closing indefinitely on April 2, 2016 to make room for the new additions.

As a sort of side note, be sure to look through YouTube at some of the videos of the experience, no matter if you get to see the show or not. As with all stunt productions, things don't always go right. Occasionally, the drivers mistime a jump or slide just a little too far, and as always, tourists have their cameras ready. You can even find videos of the roof being torn off of one of the cars that took too much speed into the final jump of the show. Thankfully, the driver was okay and immense safety precautions are in place, but these incidents can be pretty amusing.

High Octane Refreshments- Although attached to the studios Catering Co., on the park map it is listed separately which causes some confusion. The location offers a variety of alcoholic beverages that are hard to find at any other park than Epcot. Magic Kingdom only has alcohol at one location, and it is pretty limited in the other parks as well. I believe that decision is intentional on Disney's part to limit rowdy behavior from those who do not drink responsibly. Keeping that in mind, High Octane Refreshments is kind of tucked off to the side of the Catering Co., so it may take you a minute to find it. As with any Disney alcohol, there are quite a few unique offerings, but they all come with a high price tag. The drinks can be frozen if you choose as well. With all of that on the table, don't expect much from High Octane Refreshments. It is a walk up bar and not much more. Unfortunately, Disney has announced that the Catering Co. will be disappearing, but they did not specifically state that High Octane will also disappear. Of course, we can only assume so, but it could potentially be moved to a new location or developed into a food stand style experience elsewhere in the park.

The Writer's Stop- If you head back up the Streets of America, at the corner of Commissary Lane is this unique little store. Although it's not very large, it is one of the more unique shopping experiences that you can have in the Disney parks. It's basically a little Disney book store with a small case of pastries and dessert items that really bring home the local bookstore feel. Although there isn't too much to look at, the store can produce some incredible experiences for those who really enjoy Disney books. Throughout the year, there are author signings and promotional book debuts held right inside the store. If you aren't a book person, like me (Isn't that ironic!), there are a variety of little specialty items and coffee in the store that you can enjoy as well. The experience is unique, and you can't help but think about how the shop seems like a place that Walt Disney himself would have really appreciated. He always loved the little things, from the fire station on Mainstreet to the train stations. It was always the little details that made the parks special in his mind. The Writer's Shop seems to inevitably be one of those little details that really set the Disney parks apart from all other theme parks.

As I have said many times about experiences in this part of Hollywood Studios, this may be going away very soon as well. The expansion is rumored to begin at the back side of the old American Idol Experience building and then extend to the back of the park. While this does imply that the store will be going away, the Sci-Fi restaurant that is right next door seems to be staying. So, at the time of writing this book, it still stands and is open, but it does seem to be going away in the near future.

COMMISSARY LANE: Hollywood Studios has all kinds of weird little streets and cut throughs that make it a little different than most theme parks. It seems as if you have to explore in order to really find your way around the park, but it definitely makes for a fun experience. Commissary Lane is one of these little cut throughs. There isn't much there, but what is there is pretty unique and sticks to the original Hollywood theme that the park used to be focused upon.

Sci-Fi Dine-In Theatre Restaurant- The restaurant set up is incredibly clever on the part of the Disney Imagineers. When you experience it for the first time, it's a little mind blowing to be completely honest. As soon as you step in the door, you take a step back in time to drive-ins and sci-fi movies. The entire dining room area, at this table service location, is full of classic cars that are actually your table for the meal. Each car is specially made with a table top for each seating row in order to eat your meal comfortably. As you dine, the whole drive in experience comes into play. On a very large movie screen, classic sci-fi movies are played on loop that really complete the overall experience.

The food is nothing too special, but really isn't too bad. You can find about anything you would want on a menu that covers seafood, pasta, and many other american food items. The whole menu appeals to about any guest and is actually one of the largest menus in Hollywood Studios. The only real downside to the dining experience is that it's fairly hard to carry on a conversation due to the seating set up. With that being said, it really is part of the experience, but it may not be every guests' ideal dining location as a result.

ABC Commissary- The Commissary surprises a lot of guests when they first see it's name. Believe it or not, Disney has a business partnership with ABC, including the rights to the ABC name. The location is actually a counter service restaurant, and one of the rare counter service options at Hollywood Studios that is not exclusively outdoor seating. At times, the commissary can become quite crowded as a result, but it is probably the second best counter service location in the park, behind Pizza Planet. The food is pretty normal with a lot of options that are your basic, American cuisine. The design of the restaurant is pretty clever though, which makes up for its lacking creativity in food choices. When you walk in the door, it's as if you walked right into the employee cafeteria at a major production studio, as the name implies. I'm not sure how they got the design right, but the location makes you feel as if you're right in the heart of the ABC Production Studio.

MICKEY AVENUE: This section of the park isn't the most exciting to most guests and actually only features one attraction. To be honest, I think this is how the area should be. The only attraction is a museum of Walt Disney and the creation of the Disney parks, called One Man's Dream.

  One Man's Dream- As I said above, One Man's Dream isn't really an attraction, but definitely a favorite for nearly all Disney enthusiasts. The experience is like walking through the Disney Archives. The entire point is to show the creation and the goals Walt Disney set for the company and the creations that those goals brought to light. The items involved in the "museum" are incredible to see and have a distinct place in Disney history. At the end of the experience is a fairly short film, but if you wish, you can skip the film and not miss too much.

  Unfortunately, there is significant rumor that One Man's Dream is also going away sometime soon. If this comes to fruition, it will be a great loss in the parks. So many times, people go to Disney for the wrong reasons, and One Man's Dream often changed the outlook of guests before they got too far into their vacation. It makes you realize how special the parks truly are and the effort that was involved, and still is involved, in their development. Personally, I believe that if this experience goes away, the parks will lose something incredible. I understand the experience isn't in the best location, but if it is replaced, you lose the story that created the parks in the first place.

  For me, the reality of it's removal would be like removing Walt Disney from his own creation. We don't always take the time to think about where the parks came from and what made them what they are today. Sadly, Disney is starting to do the same thing at an Imagineering level to a certain extent. The goals of the parks are changing and getting away from part of the original vision and purpose. As hard as it is to believe, One Man's Dream was the first and might be the last attraction devoted to the man who had the vision to create the parks that we experience today. Due to that reason alone, it would be a real shame if it completely disappeared.

PIXAR PLACE: As the newest addition to Hollywood Studios, Pixar Place has drawn incredible crowds for months on end. Although the area is simple, the character interaction and the experiences that can be had in this extremely small section of the park are unbelievable. The entire concept is based on the look and feel of Pixar Animation Studios in Emeryville, California, but with the creative addition of the Toy Story trilogy. The decor reflects the organized chaos of Andy's bedroom. There are monkeys descending from their barrel, a Scrabble board hanging from the building, and larger than life toys strewn about. It really is an encompassing experience that leaves very little to be desired. However, it is getting an expansion in the near future with the addition of Toy Story Land, announced at the D23 expo in 2015. Although Disney has not said outright that this is the location of the expansion, it is implied with concept art and the assumption that Disney would not separate Toy Story Mania from the new Toy Story attractions.

Also, we're not sure if the theme will remain the same throughout Pixar Place. It could be redesigned to match what is being developed in the new features or it could act as a transition into the new land. Disney will probably release more details fairly soon, so be sure to be on the lookout for new information.

Toy Story Midway Mania!- The attraction itself is nothing short of a sensory overload. Before you board your ride vehicle, the sights and sounds of the experience put a huge smile on every guests face. The entire premise of the attraction is that Andy and the gang have set up a midway style target game in his bedroom. The creation that resulted from that premise is Toy Story Mania. Once you enter the queue, you realize that you're about to experience something special. The music is upbeat and entertaining and you can't help but notice a larger than life Mr. Potato head singing, dancing, and interacting with every guest that walks by. If that's not amusing enough, the actual attraction is even better.

The ride vehicle is incredibly unique and something you won't find anywhere else in the world. The set up is back to back with two guests on each side of four person vehicles. As you move through the various stages, the vehicle rotates to position each side of the vehicle in front of various 3D screens. Once the screens finish their introduction to each stage of the ride, you shoot your blaster at a series of moving targets to rack up points.

While participating in each of the various games, be sure to look for special targets throughout the scenes. Some targets trigger special effects to allow extra points to be scored, but others create an even more immersive experience with 4D effects in the form of water or air canons faced towards the ride vehicles. For example, in the scene involving the green army men, be sure to break as many of the plates that fly up from the back of the scene as you can. If you successfully break these plates with your blaster, a series of higher point value plates are thrown from below and drastically increase your score. For more tips like this one, do a simple google search for Toy Story Mania Tricks and get ready to rack up the score of the hour.

At the end of the attraction, there is a scoreboard that compares your personal score to the person sitting next to you, as well as to the other people that have played during that day and even that month. The attraction creates great friendly rivalries and can create memories in a way that so many attractions fail to do. The guest interaction is second to none and creates a desire to ride over and over again. As a result, Toy Story Mania always has an incredibly long wait that often reaches two hours or even longer during certain parts of the year. For Hollywood Studios, this is definitely a must do and a great use of a Fastpass+, if you are able to get one.

Unfortunately, there is one word of caution I have to add. If you are a person that does not do well with spinning, I cannot recommend this attraction. Although the spinning is minimal, and in no way constant, it's a warning I can't overlook. Overall, this is one of my personal favorite attractions and one that nearly everyone can enjoy.

Hey Howdy Hey Takeaway- Just outside of Toy Story Mania is this very small walk up counter service location. It doesn't offer much more than hotdogs and a few drink choices, but if you're in a pinch and really need something to eat, it will definitely fill that need. I can't really recommend eating here for any other reason. There is no seating area, and in Hollywood Studios, there is always another counter service location fairly close by.

ANIMATION COURTYARD: The animation courtyard has recently become a disappointment. The animation influence is virtually gone and one of the more creative experiences has been reimagined into something new. The rest of the courtyard is focused mainly on Disney Junior and that invokes very little interest for most adults. Fortunately and unfortunately, the courtyard is facing a lot of changes, and it's hard to believe that the changes are even close to being over with. Just as in the rest of the park, nobody quite knows what Disney's next move will be with the newly announced expansions and overwhelming construction. While I'm not too excited about the changes, the parks are constantly developing and that is something we, as Disney guests, have to always consider. The parks were never meant to be a museum, but rather an experience that is constantly developing throughout the generations.

Voyage of The Little Mermaid- The Little Mermaid show is one of the more creative ones that can be found in Walt Disney World. It isn't a very long show, but the creativity comes from the style of performance. Once everyone is seated in the theatre, the stage goes dark and black lights illuminate puppets in incredibly bright colors. Controlling the puppets are puppeteers in all black suits, so they are only vaguely visible behind the characters. It really develops an effect that very few have witnessed before and ends up being one of those clever designs that really sets Disney apart.

The entire experience is very entertaining and wonderful for kids and adults alike. Although, just like the movie, it can be scary at times, especially for very young children, it is a show that has become a favorite of guests over the years. The special effects create a distinct feeling of being under the sea through extensive use of fog machines and misting devices within the theatre. Beyond the technology, the story covers basically all aspects of the movie with some live actors thrown in the mix to further develop the on-stage production. No matter if you like the movie or not, it is almost a guarantee that you will find an element of the Voyage of The Little Mermaid to enjoy.

Disney Junior- Live On Stage!- As surprisingly one of the only attractions aimed at young children exclusively in all of the Disney parks, Disney Junior does not disappoint. The entire show features Disney Junior characters live on stage in a creative children's show. The show itself encourages kids to dance and play in a way that very few experiences do. There is no expectation for children to sit still the entire show and they are often encouraged to get involved and have a great time. The experience is extremely family friendly, but definitely focuses on the youngest of Disney parks guests. Ultimately this is a great experience, but one that fits only a certain audience. Teenagers and adults without children will not be interested in the attraction at all and will probably want to avoid it at all costs.

Over the years, the show has changed from the older characters of Bear and The Big Blue House and Stanley to a much more modern Disney Junior character group. For the kids, this is a great show that stays up to date. It has changed many times, but the ultimate goal has always been to keep adding the latest and greatest characters from children shows, which is always a struggle at the Disney parks. Thankfully, Disney has always been on top of this attraction and, as a result, it has always been a must do experience for those with young children.

Star Wars Launch Bay- Although the attraction may actually be a limited time event due to potential construction changes, it was supposedly designed to be a "permanent" location. The original idea was to create a place that Disney could add to and change as the Star Wars brand continued to evolve. Now, we don't know if that will actually happen, given that only one movie has officially debuted, but that is the plan that is supposedly in place. If the Launch Bay does remain up to date, it could end up becoming a must do attraction for all Star Wars enthusiasts!

The Launch Bay is a sort of Star Wars museum. It features your favorite, classic characters and props from the past films and the most recent film, The

Force Awakens. The entire experience is basically a walk through exhibit that took the place of the main animation themed area of the park.

Originally, this section of the Animation Courtyard allowed it to live up to it's name. The building featured a guided drawing experience with a Disney artist and functioned as a character meet and greet location as well. Often these characters were from the most recent Disney animated films and was usually the only place you could meet such characters. Additionally, this was the only place in the park to meet Sorcerer Mickey.

In my opinion, this redesign is one of the most ill considered expansions to the Hollywood Studios park. The area focused on wonderful animation stories and unique experiences that you can't find anywhere else. While Star Wars Launch Bay is incredible for those who really appreciate Star Wars, the redesign essentially removed the details of Animation from the Disney parks. In all reality, animation is what founded the parks in the first place and it seems a bit bold to deviate from their roots as a company. Don't get me wrong, there's nothing wrong with Star Wars, but it really doesn't fit in an area called Animation Courtyard.

SUNSET BOULEVARD: When most people think of Hollywood Studios, their mind automatically goes to this street. Sunset Boulevard has become iconic to the park. As home to some of the most intense and creative experiences in all of Walt Disney World, it is easy to see why it has that reputation. From Tower of Terror to Fantasmic!, there is a little something for everyone on Sunset Boulevard. However, what most people don't recognize, is that it was not a part of the park when it originally opened. For the first few years, the entire street was non existent. Considering how small Hollywood Studios feels already, I can only imagine what it was like before Sunset Boulevard. Even though the guest expectations weren't quite the same then, it is something that is a little strange to think about, especially considering all that is a part of the street today.

Starring Rolls Cafe- Right next to the Hollywood Brown Derby is this creative little cafe, just steps from the corner of Sunset Boulevard. The cafe is a great place to use a snack credit on the dining plan or even catch a light breakfast early on in your day at Hollywood Studios. Unfortunately, the menu is fairly similar to the Trolley Car Café across the street, but does not feature Starbucks coffee.

Throughout the day, Starring Rolls also offers a few light sandwiches and is a great place to eat a light meal, especially after a larger, table service meal at lunch. The cafe is a counter service location, but does not have extensive menu options. The main focus is pastries and baked goods rather than full meals, but you could always create your own meal with various pastries! Additionally, the location isn't really set up for extensive guest traffic. There is no interior seating and the seating that is available is outdoors and fairly limited. Without question, this is a great place to stop in for a quick snack, but I would definitely look into the other near by options if you're looking for an entire meal.

Sweet Spells- As the flagship candy store in the studios, Sweet Spells leaves a little to be desired. The freshly made items that range from chocolate dipped marshmallows to fudge and candy apples are wonderful, but the other packaged candies aren't much to write home about. The items are still good in the packages, but they are basically the same as what you would find at any of your local grocery stores, but with the Disney branding and a much higher price. The options in the case that are freshly made are all very tasty, but also carry a fairly lofty price tag as well. At the other end of the store are a few collectibles and villains t-shirts that fit the villains theme of the entire store. No matter how many times you visit this location, it pails in comparison to the confectionary on Main Street U.S.A. in the Magic Kingdom.

Beauty and the Beast- Live on Stage- We all know the story of the tale as old as time, but the stage show brings the story to life, right in front of your eyes. With live actors singing and dancing on stage, the experience is like being at a small-scale Broadway play. The story is very familiar, as it should be, for anyone who has seen the movie, but the performers are very good at what they do and the entire show portrays the movie in song and dance. The audience for this experience is pretty self explanatory. If you like the movie, I'm sure you will love the stage show. If you don't like the movie and don't like singing and dancing, this probably isn't the attraction for you. If you are one of those people, don't worry, there are many things you can do nearby while the rest of your group enjoys the show.

The Twilight Zone Tower of Terror- If you are like most guests, then you may realize that the Twilight Zone was never a part of Disney or ABC productions. As a result, the attraction is actually contracted through CBS for rights to the name, but the whole licensing situation is actually quite complicated.

The Tower of Terror attraction features a haunted elevator and an equally haunting story. I won't ruin the story for you, because it is actually a huge part of the attraction, but I will say the experience ends with a broken elevator and an exciting conclusion. Although it is categorized as family friendly, it definitely only appeals to a select audience of thrill seekers. In addition to the ride being fairly intense, it can actually be quite scary for younger guests. However, if you are a thrill seeker, be prepared for a new attraction to add to your list of favorites.

After the thrills are over, be sure to look through the merchandise location as you exit. The items found in the store are not available many other places on property and actually feature the Hollywood Tower name. You can even buy the service bell from the front desk! Why buy the classic tourist, yearly, dated, shirts when you can buy something that you can attach to a specific memory. I say the same thing about all of the unique merchandise locations at all of the parks, but it really is something fun to consider.

Rock 'n' Roller Coaster Starring Aerosmith- Rock 'n' Roller Coaster falls into a very similar category to that of Tower of Terror. It has a main story and a borrowed brand through the Aerosmith label, but the attraction is completely different in design. Rock 'n' Roller Coaster is quite possibly the most intense experience out of all of the Disney parks world wide. The coaster is almost completely free of big free fall drops, but the speed comes from a electronic launching mechanism that is one of the most advanced ever developed.

From the moment the attraction begins, you know you're in for a thrill. The starting mechanism features a 0-60mph launch in under 3 seconds into nearly complete darkness. The rest of the attraction is almost completely dark and filled with all kinds of inversions and other thrill inducing aspects. As you can imagine, this is one for the ultimate thrill seeker. Creatively, the attraction also has a unique themed aspect that ties in the Aerosmith label. Before you even board the ride vehicle, a pre-show informs you that you are invited to an Aerosmith concert by the band themselves, but you'll have to hurry to get there.

Just through the doors, your super stretch limo awaits. As the pre-show mentioned, you might be late so the limo peels out of the drive at break neck speeds and your wild adventure to the venue begins. Oh, and I forgot to mention, your super stretch has some extremely loud speakers that blare Aerosmith classics all the way to the venue. At the end of the ride, you get to the venue and exit through one of the most unique merchandise locations on property. Aerosmith products are everywhere and, after making it through that experience, you will definitely want something to remember it by.

Sunset Ranch Market- The market area is probably the most extensive compilation of food locations that you can find anywhere at Walt Disney World. If you can't find something good to eat here, you aren't trying hard enough. The entire area is very similar to an actual marketplace. There are fresh fruit areas, the iconic turkey leg stand, burgers, chicken, and even pizza locations spread out across a large outdoor seating area. Outdoor seating here can be a little hectic at times, but Sunset Ranch really does have something to please nearly any guest preference.

Fantasmic!- Each of the Disney parks have a special nighttime show that ends out the night and sends each and every guest home with a big smile on their face. Fantasmic! is that experience at Hollywood Studios. The show is very difficult to explain, but extremely popular. The best explanation that I can give is that it is water affects, fireworks, and on stage performances, all combined to create a spectacular show.

The stadium style seating is all outdoors and often fills up very quickly. Be sure to get there at least 30-45 minutes in advance to even have a shot at a seat during the peak seasons. On most nights, there are 2 different shows, one earlier on in the night and one later, usually after the rest of the park closes. Seating is given on a first come, first serve basis, and the best seats are always taken first. The only exception to the rule is if you get the Fantasmic! dinner package at Hollywood and Vine.

Recently, there has been a simple addition of sorts to the show. The experience has been expanded through the "glow with the show" merchandise which started out at California Adventure with World of Color. The technology has been adopted here in Hollywood Studios and is starting to catch on. Basically, it allows a purchased set of Mickey ears, which have colorful lighting built in, to blink along with everyone else in the audience as the show progresses. The effect creates a sea of color and really encompasses the guests in the magic of the show. No matter what your day has been like in Hollywood Studios, I can guarantee it will end with a bang at Fantasmic!

As you can probably see, there are a lot of changes coming to the studios and, surprisingly, that is nothing new for the park. The experience in the studios has always been changing, but now the park seems to have a new focus that will give the experiences a new, immersive element. Although it's hard to see some of the classics going away, it's always good to see Walt Disney World growing and developing for our future enjoyment. If things never change, they can never get better! You can't keep doing the same thing and expect a different result and, fortunately, Disney is beginning to take note of that throughout their entire group of theme park destinations.

I understand your favorite attractions, if you are a returning guest, may no longer be there, but be sure to give the studios a second chance in the future. Some people see this as a half day park in its current state, which is completely understandable, but I can still guarantee there will always be something you've never experienced left to do. As I have mentioned time after time in this book, exploring the parks is an adventure and you can never see and do everything. That idea is what keeps us coming back, and even though you may never see it all, you can always experience even more of what the parks have to offer!

DISNEY'S ANIMAL KINGDOM

OASIS: I'm not even going to try to cover it up, I'm really not the biggest fan of Animal Kingdom. The park doesn't have that same magical feeling as the other Disney parks for one reason or another. Part of that could be due to the fact that sections function as a small scale zoo, but I believe the larger contributor is the incredible amount of walking the park requires in order to do very little. Now don't get me wrong, I understand walking a lot is a huge part of a Disney vacation, but there is no reason Animal Kingdom had to be so spread out! The Oasis is a great example. The entire area of the park has one restaurant (that you don't even need a ticket to the park to eat at) and a gift shop. The rest of it is just a walkway with a couple animals scattered around the trail in little blocked off areas. Everyone must enter and leave through the Oasis, and it really lacks that wow factor that each of the other park entrances have.

Rainforest Cafe- Yep, you read that right. There is a chain restaurant in Animal Kingdom. I used to love Rainforest Cafe just as much as any other kid, but I expect a little more creativity on Disney's part to develop a once in a lifetime experience. The only good part of the restaurant is that you don't really have to have a ticket to the park to eat there. Technically, both entrances to the restaurant are outside of the park. With that being said, if you have friends or family that want to meet up for lunch or dinner and don't want to pay for an extra day in the parks or who don't want to go to the parks, they can always join you for a meal at Rainforest Cafe. If I was going to do that, I have to suggest the Rainforest Cafe at Disney Springs instead. The location at the springs is much more exciting and features an "active" volcano. It is quite possibly the best of all the Rainforest Cafe's nation wide.

With that being said, sometimes that choice isn't always available. However, don't expect much out of the food. It isn't bad food, but it definitely isn't much better than any other restaurant chain's offerings. That really wouldn't be bad, but the prices they charge are ridiculous for the quality of the items being served. I understand you're paying for the building, theming, and special effects, but at least make the food worth the price. Some people really enjoy the restaurant, but with so many better options in the park, it is extremely hard to recommend Rainforest Cafe even though I have eaten there many times.

Garden Gate Gifts- This little gift shop is definitely one that is used by guests who forgot something cheap, but somewhat important for their day at the park. For example, when I was much younger, I forgot my sunglasses at the resort and needed a quick replacement to avoid the trip back. Garden Gate Gifts fixed the issue and we were on our way. Other than fixing those little incidents, don't expect much more out of the merchandise found at this location. Originally, it had a greater role as a camera center when cameras still primarily used film. Today, as you can imagine, that service is virtually never needed. Overall, if you can't find it here, don't worry. There is a much larger gift shop just across the bridge on Discovery Island.

As a quick note, if you ever do find yourself in one of these situations, each park has a store very similar to Garden Gate Gifts near the front entrance. At Epcot, it's directly under Spaceship Earth, at Magic Kingdom, there is one at ticket and transportation, but also one at the front of the park near the gates, and at Hollywood Studios, it is on your left hand side of the entrances. You never know when you'll forget something small, but important enough to be needed for your day in the parks. You may pay more at these little stores for what you need, but sometimes it's better than missing a fastpass+ or dining reservation that you scheduled far in advance.

DISCOVERY ISLAND: Personally, I believe this is where the entrance of the park should have been. Nothing really happens at Animal Kingdom until you cross over the bridge onto Discovery Island. The Island, featuring the iconic Tree of Life, creates that wow factor that the other parks have front and center.

Discovery Island acts like the hub (the area where the partners statue is) in Magic Kingdom. It is the center of the park and a gateway to all the other lands of Animal Kingdom. If you ever get lost in the park, ask a cast member or find your way back to Discovery Island and you can get anywhere from there with the many directional signs scattered around the island.

Wilderness Explorers- You may recognize the name here from the hugely popular Pixar film, UP. Russell, one of the main characters in the film, was termed a Wilderness Explorer. For those of you who have not seen the movie, a Wilderness Explorer is someone who is a friend of all nature, similar to a boy scout. There is no better place to learn and experience nature than in the Animal Kingdom. The experience focuses on this idea, and Disney has developed a scavenger hunt of locations to find that starts here, but spreads throughout the park. If you are a first time guest, especially if you have young children, this is a great way to explore a little bit of everything the park has to offer at no additional cost. The entire "attraction" is self guided and at your own pace, so you can see as much or as little as you would like. While there is a Wilderness Explorers starting location in each of the lands across Animal Kingdom, this location is one of the best starting points, because it is often the first one you come to in the park.

Island Mercantile- The only real comparison I can make to this merchandise location, would be that it is similar, but also very different from the Emporium in Magic Kingdom. It is the largest store in the park and offers a wide variety of merchandise that is largely unique to Animal Kingdom. Just like the Emporium, if you can't find what you're looking for here, you are probably going to have a hard time finding it anywhere else in the park.

It's Tough to Be a Bug!- If you ever had the opportunity to see Honey, I Shrunk the Audience! at Epcot, this is pretty much the same type of attraction. It is a theatre that interacts with the guests in various ways as the short film on screen progresses. It's Tough to Be a Bug is focused on the characters from the Bug's Life movie. Once seated in the Tree of Life theatre, the audience is fully involved with the show, which can be good and bad, depending on your preferences.

Throughout the production, there are simulated feelings of bugs running under your feet and even a bee sting that really grabs your attention. For some guests, this is extremely entertaining, but others despise the attraction due to the interaction. Because of those elements, it is really hard to pin down a certain audience for the attraction. Guests of all ages can attend the show, but some may not necessarily enjoy it.

As strange as it may sound, one of the best elements of the actual attraction experience is the theatre itself. It looks and feels as if it is actually underneath of the Tree of Life, the icon of the park. The Imagineer creativity and artistic ability is obvious and it really adds to an experience that is enveloping to begin with. It really is hard to tell that the tree is made of a simulated material created to take on the characteristics of a real, living tree.

Adventurer's Outpost- In Animal Kingdom, it seems as if every character has a unique, wilderness outfit. Mickey and Minnie are no different. Dressed in their safari gear, ready for an adventure, Mickey and Minnie interact with guests and sign autographs in front of a creative backdrop. Unlike most parks, character interaction here is rarely limited to just one character. For most guests, this is a great aspect of the outpost. You can get your picture taken with Mickey and Minnie at the same time, which is quite rare when it comes to character interaction.

Surprisingly, the wait time varies drastically. Some parts of the day, the line is backed up, while other times, you will only wait a few minutes. Unfortunately, the wait is fairly difficult to predict. The best thing to do in a situation like this is to keep checking back to see if the wait time has gone down. Most of the time, you will catch a break in the crowds sometime throughout the day and will minimize your time standing in line.

Flame Tree Barbecue- Growing up in Kentucky, I am no stranger to good barbecue. Surprisingly, the barbecue in the Disney parks nearly always meets or surpasses my expectations. Flame Tree Barbecue is no different. If for some reason you do not eat barbecue, Flame Tree also has many other options, so there is always something on the menu for nearly every guest. While being a counter service location, it still offers a clever seating design that creates a wonderful atmosphere. The seating is completely outdoors, but is mostly covered. However, the views are what create the wow factor.

Just off the back balcony, the view of Expedition Everest is quite possibly the best view in the park. Although The Tree of Life is the true icon of the park, Everest is becoming a close second. The level of detail put into the design and perspective of the mountain is unbelievable. The outdoor seating at Flame Tree allows you to take in the view and really admire that extreme detail that sets Disney Imagineering apart. I understand I have said that so many times throughout the book, but it really is something you have to see to believe.

When I was younger, I never quite took the time to recognize all of the subtle details the Disney company puts into each and every project they create. If you take the time to pause in your vacation and step back for a minute, the magic of Disney really sets in. Sadly, most guests are so focused on the next attraction or the next thing on their list that they don't take time to admire the beauty around them. Some of the greatest memories I have at Walt Disney World are in these moments of doing nothing. Take ten minutes or so to sit on a bench and look around for the details that make the parks so special. What you observe may astound you. Watch the smiles on your friends and families faces throughout your vacation and cherish those moments. It really is the small things that you will remember from your Disney vacation when you get home and by stepping back and slowing down from time to time, you really get to take in the full spectrum of the Disney Magic.

The Smiling Crocodile and Eight Spoon Cafe- There are two kiosks remarkably close to Flame Tree Barbecue which both offer counter service food as well. However, when you're this close to Flame Tree, you might as well go there instead. Neither of the kiosks have a seating area, and the only place the menus really excel are in the various snack type options offered. If you're not looking for a full meal, you may want to check out these stands. But, if you want an actual counter service meal, be sure to look into Flame Tree Barbecue or Pizzafari which are both just a short walk away.

Terra Treats- While this may not be a great dining location for every guest, it is a necessity and incredibly helpful for other guests. Terra Treats is a part of a continuous effort by Disney to accommodate those with allergies or dietary restrictions. It offers some food of its own that is usually gluten and allergy friendly, but also functions as an information station for dining guidance for those with allergies. In a park with fairly diverse menus, this was really a necessity on Disney's part and they faced the challenge head on.

While this service doesn't exist in all of the Disney parks to my knowledge, never be afraid to ask to speak to a chef about allergy concerns at any dining location. From personal experience with friends and family, Disney will do just about anything to accommodate allergies of all types. Most of the time, at table service meals, the chef will actually come to your table and either personally explain to you what you are able to eat on the existing menu or offer to make you something special. To most peoples' surprise, the chefs actually seem to honestly enjoy the opportunity to make a guest something special. It seems to give them a reason to exhibit their culinary skills and get away from their normal repetitive creation of standard menu items. Often times, the specially created items are even better than the standard menu items. Also, getting the opportunity to interact with and enjoy a personalized creation from some of Disney's world-class chefs is a wonderful and memorable experience for everyone involved with the meal.

Pizzafari- In a park full of adventurous offerings in the way of food as well as attractions, it's always nice to have a place to go to get a simple meal. How much simpler does it get than pizza? While pizza is the main item on the Pizzafari menu, there are a few other offerings as well. In late 2015, the menu changed slightly, but it appears as if a majority of the menu is nearly identical to what it used to be. If you have already read my description of the food at Pizza Planet or have been to Pizza Planet yourself, the food at Pizzafari is incredibly similar. Both locations have pizza that tastes nearly identical and the only major difference is in the way of obvious theming elements. If you liked Pizza Planet, you will most definitely enjoy Pizzafari and the same is true in reverse. As you probably already know, Pizza Planet is my personal favorite counter service location at Hollywood Studios, so it should come as no surprise that I highly recommend Pizzafari as well.

Creature Comforts- As a part of the Starbucks additions to every Disney park, Creature Comforts serves as that location in the Animal Kingdom. While the location used to be a merchandise area, the building underwent immense construction and redesign to create a coffee shop environment with a distinctly African flair. Similar to the Trolley Car at Hollywood Studios and the Mainstreet

130

Bakery in Magic Kingdom, the menu features a few simple pastries and, of course, Starbucks coffee. The entire Starbucks menu is not present at any of the in-park locations, but many of the more popular offerings are on the menu. As with many other bakeries and coffee locations on property, there is no seating area and after leaving the pickup counter, you have to wander the park or find a bench to eat whatever you purchased. Of course, you always have the option to eat on top of a trash can which has, surprisingly, become a good option at Disney, especially during festivals. Don't worry, most of the trashcans are surprisingly clean, but it wouldn't hurt Disney to create a few more seating areas near dining locations.

Disney Outfitters- If for some reason you can't find what you're looking for at the Island Mercantile, this is your next best option. The difference between the two is that Disney Outfitters offers more of the African-inspired merchandise. While they both are very large and feature a lot of the same items, Disney Outfitters seems to be the more crowded store, due to it's location. Just as with the Island Mercantile, if you can't find what you're looking for here, you probably won't find it anywhere else in the park unless it is directly related to an attraction. Between the two locations many offerings, you can find just about any Animal Kingdom merchandise that you could ever want. The Animal Kingdom has some of the more unique souvenirs that aren't in any of the other parks, so be sure to at least stroll through these stores if you have a little extra time. You never know what you may find and want to take home with you.

Just beyond the store and before crossing the bridge over into DinoLand USA, keep your eyes open for a little perch off to the right. At certain times throughout the day, there is a short little show here that is amazing to see. Personally, I never took the time to watch the show until my last visit, but now, it is on my list of must do events. Don't expect a grand spectacle with an elaborate stage or anything, but it will blow you away.

The show starts with a group of trained Disney cast members and they explain that a group of birds will be arriving soon as they do everyday. What you don't expect though, is that those birds will be flying in on their own and leaving on their own! As shocking as it is the first time you see it, it really is incredible to watch. You look down the street of the park filled with guests and, all of a sudden, a big swarm of various tropical birds swoop down from above and land on the perch right in front of you. The cast members interact with the birds for a few minutes and take questions. Then, like clockwork, they can countdown to when the birds will leave. Part of their explanation in the show is that the birds do this every single day, unguided. Surprisingly, this experience moves to other areas of the park for construction and special events, and the birds still show up somehow. This simple creation really is one that blows your mind the first time you see it and really goes to show the extent to which Disney theming extends. I can virtually guarantee that no other theme park has exotic birds that fly freely through their amusement park.

AFRICA: Originally, the Africa area of Animal Kingdom was actually destined to be one of the pavilions in the World Showcase at Epcot Center. When the plans for the Showcase were physically developed, the Africa pavilion was scrapped for a few reasons. The general assumption is that the Imagineers and Disney executives realized the potential the pavilion held and decided to move forward with an entire theme park based on the concept. Today, Africa is one the most diversely themed lands out of all the Disney parks, and it continues to grow.

While the area often faced criticism for stereotypical images of Africa, the more recent developments virtually eliminate those problems. Recently, changes have come to the area that give it a restored sense of authenticity and increased guest interaction with an all new dining experience. These changes mark the beginning of a transformation of Animal Kingdom from a day time park to a full scale day and night park.

For those of you who are new to Disney, Animal Kingdom, in the past, has always closed much earlier than the other parks on a daily basis. Sometimes, that could be as early as 5:00 or 6:00pm. Disney has always explained that the reason for the early closing times was due to the animals and their specific needs. However, Disney has recently launched a campaign to make Animal Kingdom a nighttime, as well as a daytime, park. To do so, Disney is working on an entirely new area of the park where Camp Minnie-Mickey once was.

In the area being developed, James Cameron's imaginary land of Pandora will come to life. Here, there will be a new series of attractions based on the Avatar film, as well as a completely immersive environment that Disney Imagineering has worked alongside James Cameron himself to develop. From artist renderings and models presented at the D23 expo this year, it appears as if Pandora could be the most immersive experience to date. In addition to Pandora, Imagineering has been working to create a new nighttime experience exclusively for Animal Kingdom named 'Rivers of Light'.

From the conceptual artwork, the experience seems to be similar to a mix of World of Color, from Disney's California Adventure, and Fantasmic!, from both Disneyland and Hollywood Studios. Although the show will have a unique flare, it will be interesting to see how Disney incorporates the show in a way that will not disturb the animals. From what Disney claims, that is the current explanation for why there is no nighttime spectacular in Animal Kingdom. As you can clearly see, Africa is just the beginning of the expansions, and an effort to revitalize the Animal Kingdom for future guest enjoyment.

Festival of The Lion King- Who doesn't love The Lion King? The music was incredible, the animation was just as perfect, and Disney has expanded on everything it brings to the table with the Festival of The Lion King. When you enter the theatre, you will realize a few things. First, the theatre appears quite small, and second it is unlike any theater you have ever seen before. Unlike a traditional Broadway theatre, the stage is in the center of the floor and the bleacher style seating surrounds it. Once the show begins, the clever seating design begins to make sense. Thanks to the semi-circular setup, the performers are able to fill the room with an incredible display of singing, dancing, and animatronics that rival some of the best shows on Broadway.

When finding your seat, be sure to get there very early for the best seats or at the last minute to end up with an end seat. Although that sounds a little strange, I will explain. There really is no bad seat in the theatre, but if you have kids, it is best to sit down front or on one of the ends for a chance at a special opportunity to join in the show. During the second to last song of the performance, the room fills with singers, stilt walkers, tumble monkeys, and even a fire dancer. As a part of this elaborate display, members of the show pick a group of about six children to go out on stage and play instruments with them. From personal experience as a kid, it is something really neat to be involved with. I wouldn't be writing about it today if I didn't remember it, so it's easy to say that this experience could stick with you forever.

As for the actual show itself, it has a sort of nudge to the Lion King series of movies with characters from the films, but is more of a representation of the Lion King concept rather than a run through the movie. Disney took a risk on this show and made it something unique and more of a performance rather than a reproduction of the films. The risk paid off big time and created one the most wonderful and memorable shows you will ever find. Throughout the act, there are incredibly talented singers that have performed here for years, acrobats that are some of the most talented in the world, and you can't forget all of the Lion King characters that are also in the mix. When it comes down to it, you will be hard pressed to find a more enjoyable show.

What comes as a surprise for many is that the Festival of the Lion King recently relocated to the Africa portion of the park. Originally, the show had a role in the Camp Minnie-Mickey area, but with the recent construction of Pandora, the show was relocated. The new location is almost identical to the old one with the exception of a designated queue area that is much better than the last one. The new location may actually be bigger, or at least it appears so from the outside. Most of the onstage areas are basically identical, but I can only assume the backstage areas are larger and more elaborate than they were in the past. No matter what the location is like, be sure to experience the Festival of The Lion King on your next adventure in the Animal Kingdom.

Donald's Dining Safari at Tusker House- When Animal Kingdom comes to mind, character meals are not the first thing most people think of. Tusker House is the rare and single exception to that idea. It's the only character meal in the park, so it shouldn't come as a surprise that it's popular among families.

As a table service credit on the dining plan, this location offers a little bit of everything by means of an expansive buffet serving breakfast, lunch, and dinner. A majority of the breakfast menu is centered around American offerings, but the other meals feature a creative African flair throughout the same buffet environment. No different than most Disney character experiences, with the exception of Hollywood and Vine, the character interaction is great and allows the guests to interact with Donald Duck and friends. Each of the characters are dressed in their safari attire in order to match the restaurants' elaborate theming and truly immerse the guest in the Tusker House environment.

When looking at the physical setup of the building, it features a series of rooms, all representing a different piece of the African design elements. Due to the setup, there are a variety of experiences that can be had at Tusker House just by being seated in different rooms. Ultimately, it gives the restaurant a greater repeat value. While the main seating is indoors, there is also a clever outdoor seating area that is themed quite well. I understand some people prefer eating outdoors, but the Florida heat doesn't always make that the best possible experience. Hopefully, with the development of Animal Kingdom into a nighttime park as well as a daytime park, the outdoor seating will become an interesting option after the sun goes down.

The overwhelming response to Tusker House recently has been quite positive, but be aware that the park often closes early in the day, so dinner reservations may not always be the best use of your time. Many guests finish up their day in Animal Kingdom by mid afternoon, then use the park hopper option to move on to another park. You never want to waste time sitting around for hours just waiting on a reservation. At Walt Disney World, time is your friend and the more of it you can save, the more you can see and do during your vacation! While the restaurant may not be your best option for later dining, breakfast is quite popular, and reservations are fairly readily available if you book in advance. The dining experience is good overall and great for families, but only if it fits into your plan for the parks.

Kilimanjaro Safaris- It's a rare occasion when you can get off of an attraction and really feel like you could ride it over and over again with a completely new and different experience. The safaris are one of those occasions for so many reasons. The entire attraction is based on the concept of embarking on an expedition through the Harambe Wildlife Reserve, which brings a little bit of Africa to central Florida! As you can imagine, Disney went above and beyond to make the experience authentic. To do so, they pulled out all of the stops and created a ride vehicle like no other. To embark on your safari, you enter a custom made truck fitted with multiple speakers and driven by a Safari guide.

Once your journey begins, your guide, who is also also your driver, sets the scene and pilots your vehicle through various terrain while spotting animals along the way. The attraction is constantly changing due to the experience being reliant on real life animals and due to that factor, some of the best pictures at Walt Disney World come from Kilimanjaro Safaris. Personally, I have almost been licked by a giraffe and a rhino blocked our vehicles' path for several minutes during a past journey. You never know what to expect from Kilimanjaro Safaris, and that's really what makes it such an incredible attraction. Once you pair that with the music and animosity of the various guides, it becomes an attraction that should never be overlooked.

One thing that must be said and will be repeated multiple times while on the attraction is that you must be very careful not to lose any cameras or belongings while in your vehicle. The vehicles will not stop for any reason for the safety of both the guests and the driver, because the animals are allowed to roam free to a certain extent. Of course, the lions can't get to the giraffes and so on, but the fact of the matter is that if you drop your camera and they stop to get it, there is always the off chance that a rhino will decide to charge. While that isn't likely, and all the more dangerous animals are unable to get near the vehicle, you definitely don't want to lose a camera or cell phone during your adventure. A second word of caution is for those who get motion sick very easily. While the drivers are quite good, the terrain is incredibly rough and you will get bounced around the entire ride. Nearly all parts of the attraction are at a slow pace, but if you are very sensitive to motion, you may want to sit this one out.

If you have been on Kilimanjaro Safaris before, you should be informed that it isn't quite the same as it used to be. The overall concept of the attraction is identical, but the section involving the rescue of Little Red from poachers has been completely removed. It's removal took away the higher speed section of the attraction, but also provided area for new animals to roam. The new sections already include zebras from time to time, but unfortunately, when the zebras were first introduced to their simulated habitat it didn't go exactly as planned. Drivers often claimed that they were misbehaving, but we can take that to mean one of two things. Either they had a zebra get out of its designated space somehow or they did not do well in the space physically.

The second addition, soon to be added to the safari, is in the way of wild dogs. It will be interesting to see how this implementation is made, but it could make for a new and original idea. As you can probably imagine, Kilimanjaro Safari appeals to just about every guest and often has some incredibly long wait times. The trick for managing the wait is to get in line within the first hour or two of when the park opens for the day. The lines always move significantly faster in the morning since nothing has had the opportunity to slow down the pace of those in the queue. If you don't intend to be there when the park opens, I highly recommend using a fastpass+.

If you do use the fastpass+ option, be sure to try to book the attraction during the sunrise in the morning or during the sunset in the evening. While this sounds a bit strange, often times the animals are much more active during these time periods and the scenery really takes on a whole different set of characteristics as well. The sunrise over the savannah really feels authentic in a way that is a bit hard to describe, but really quite amazing to witness. In the same regard, pictures turn out much better at these times due to the more elaborate backdrops created by the colorful sky. Of course, it's always a luck of the draw, but it's great to have a little something extra to look forward to during your day in the Animal Kingdom.

Pangani Forest Exploration Trail- If you're still looking to see even more animals, this is the largest animal viewing trail in the park. The entire trail is a small-scale zoo environment. When you combine all of the different animals found at the various trails throughout the park, you essentially have a zoo as well as a theme park to explore. Pangani Forest focuses on African animals, such as gorillas and hippos which are very entertaining to watch. Although those aren't the only animals on the trail, they are the main highlights of the quick little walk around area. In my own opinion, the various trails across the park aren't the best use of your time, but if you really enjoy animals, you may want to take the extra time to explore them.

Kusafiri Coffee Shop and Bakery- On the corner, directly across from the entrance to Kilimanjaro Safaris is this little walk-up window. The location offers a variety of pastries for breakfast as well as coffee. After the breakfast time is finished, Kusafiri also meets your needs for sweets and various dessert items throughout the day. If that description sounds familiar, that's because the new Starbucks location, Creature Comforts, offers an almost identical range of products. Given that these dining options are not very far apart, the only definitive reason you should choose one over the other would be your preference in coffee.

Each of the Starbucks locations added to the parks seem to be in the same scenario. Either Starbucks replaced an existing option with an almost identical menu, or you can get the same items near by at another location. To me that makes it obvious that adding Starbucks to the park was a marketing ploy rather than an honest addition. To be completely honest, that's probably where my irritation with the branding comes from. I completely understand that brand names have always been in the park for sponsorship and various food items, such as Dole Whip, but don't try to fix something that isn't broken in the first place. The best example of this is at Mainstreet Bakery in Magic Kingdom.

The bakery had a sort of legacy on Mainstreet as a place to grab a dessert before the parade, or breakfast upon entering the park, but once Starbucks took over and the location was redesigned, it lost part of it's legacy. The seating where you could hear the parade and listen to the music of it passing by outside the windows is gone and will never return. The classic bakery atmosphere is gone and all the opportunities and memories the space provided for so many guests for so many years disappeared with the atmosphere. Today, we have a location that holds no truly special experience. Starbucks is a wonderful company, but to me, it has no real purpose in the parks. I have a Starbucks three miles from my house, so there's nothing special about it anymore.

Overall, I just feel as if Disney could have done, and have been doing so much better with their own creations. Kusafiri is a great example of just that idea. The location is simple, but creatively themed, and offers anything you could really want or need out of a Starbucks style restaurant. Why would you need to build a new restaurant and destroy a perfectly good merchandise location one hundred yards away just to slap a brand name on a product that already exists? Disney has done a lot of things right in the parks over the years, but I think they made a poor decision in this scenario. As with anything, people will disagree with me, but if you're looking for breakfast, be sure to look into Kusafiri Coffee Shop and Bakery before just running to the Starbucks name.

Harambe Fruit Market- With that little Starbucks rant out of the way, we can move on to what happens when Disney displays their creativity, no matter how simple of a form it comes in. The fruit market is very similar to the Liberty Square Market at Magic Kingdom. In all reality, it is just a fruit cart, but fruit is often times a welcomed change after spending a few days in the Disney parks. It seems like every restaurant you go to serves heavy or fried food, so having some fresh fruit one morning or afternoon, or any time really, can give you a little extra energy. Fruit items are always incredibly fresh, ripe, and ready to go. In addition to the great quality, the prices aren't too extreme, which actually comes as a surprise to most guests.

Although all of these things are good, the way the location is set apart is due to the theming that matches the environment. You can't help but feel like you're in a tiny little fruit market picking out fresh produce in Africa. In a way, it feels like a side of the road fruit stand, but at the same time, it feels fresh and new. These little details are where the creativity of Disney really thrives. Creativity is what makes experiences special and unique, not necessarily slapping a brand on a new merchandise location. While the Fruit Market is actually sponsored by Ocean Spray, you would never know it unless you looked for it on the park map. For me, I think that's exactly how it should be in a Disney park. The branding is getting a little out of hand, but at the same time, Disney's obvious goal of immersing guests in unique environments is growing. The two things don't always go hand in hand, and hopefully that becomes obvious in the future.

Harambe Market- Continuing on with immersive environments, Harambe Market is the latest and greatest addition to Animal Kingdom. The time, money, and attention to detail put into, not only the atmosphere, but also the menu items, is really astonishing. Considering it's status as a counter service location, the theming throughout the market outdoes its price point. While not the cheapest of counter service food, the meal options are fairly reasonable in price and of great quality. The entire setup is similar to an outdoor food court due to the fact that it features many walk up style locations sharing a common dining area. However, the big difference is in the atmosphere. Harambe Market is incredibly themed and matches its surroundings in a very clever way, even though the rest of the area was built many years ago.

In the market itself, there is plenty of seating and a variety of menu items, each with a distinctly African, but still recognizably American flavor. As strange as that sounds, the best way to explain it is through the example of the corndogs served in the market. The flavor is more bold than an American style corndog, but the item is still appealing to a mostly American audience. To achieve the distinct flavor, the batter is infused with curry and really delivers a one of a kind, unexpected taste.

Getting back to the atmosphere, Disney has created a very unique environment. The train, which is used as transportation to Rafiki's Planet Watch, in the background sets the stage for the hustle and bustle of the marketplace atmosphere. Additionally, the staged scenario is set up with little displays of African art being sold to the patrons of the market, and a majority of it is either African or Disney's recreation of African pieces. Surprisingly, Disney uses the displays solely as props and do not attempt to actually sell the items. Believe it or not, a significant amount of research has been put into the design of the dining locations. Not only did Disney go and research in various countries, but they took the extra steps involved to recreate a fairly authentic experience. From food to atmosphere, you really can't go wrong with this cleverly themed dining option. For a park that has very few counter service options to start with, Harambe Market is a wonderful new addition to the offerings found throughout Animal Kingdom.

Tamu Tamu Refreshments- From what I understand, Tamu Tamu has recently transitioned from a counter service dining location to a strictly dessert and Dole Whip counter. (I know all the Dole Whip fans got excited when they read that!) Yes, the wonderful dessert can now be found in a third location at Walt Disney World, and I couldn't be happier. Originally, the location was one that I personally had never visited, but with the recent change, I will be sure to stop by next time I'm over that way. Surprisingly, and contrary to most locations serving the iconic frozen creation, there is actually other dessert options unrelated to pineapple offered here as well. If you're looking for a good dessert in Africa, make sure to take a look at Tamu Tamu. The changes do not really come as a surprise to me, and I can only imagine it is a result of the plans that developed into the Harambe Market near by. With all of the food choices offered a few steps away, it's great to see Disney taking the initiative to transform the menu into something that most guests will really enjoy.

Dawa Bar- This little bar is one of the more clever on property, but is often overlooked. Under an outdoor, shaded area that really carries the theming, you can order a variety of specialty alcoholic drinks. Every part of the experience is unique, but not really over the top creative. The cocktails are fairly diverse, but the biggest draw to the bar would have to be the availability of actual African beers. For some people, it is quite fun to try the various offerings, but I can imagine the Dawa Bar will begin to draw more considerable crowds as Animal Kingdom makes the transition into an all day park. With the current time schedule for Animal Kingdom on most days, a majority of people are not in the mood for a cocktail at lunch time. As always, if that's what you like to do, Disney will open up that opportunity and that's one of the best tricks to enjoying the parks. Find what you like to do and stick to it. You don't have to ride rides to have a great time. If you like to eat, drink, golf, fish, ride rides, Disney has you covered, and the list goes on and on. There really is something for everyone. The adventure is finding what you love to do and seeing how Disney's world-class accommodations fit into your vacation.

Mombasa Marketplace- Other than a few fun kiosk style stands, Mombasa is really your only major merchandise location in Africa. As strange as that is compared to sections of most Disney parks, the merchandise area is one that I rarely walk right past. Every time you go in to shop or just look around, there is always something new and unique. Just outside the door, there are various artists and craftsman that create some of the items within the store. Although there are simple t-shirts and other trinket items, the best part is finding those items with a sort of personal touch. Many of the things being sold, you can observe being made.

Just like the World Showcase merchandise, the experience creates a story that accompanies your purchase, no matter how big or small. Everything from elaborate carved walking sticks to small wooden animals can be found and purchased, nearly all of which have been hand made at some point. (Be sure to use package delivery or pickup for larger items!) It's not often that you get to witness a product being created, so having that opportunity makes Mombassa Marketplace somewhere that I always check out while waiting for a fastpass+ time or just to explore with a few extra minutes.

Wildlife Express Train- The train is really more of a means of transportation rather than an attraction, but it often varies from guest to guest. Some people really like to ride trains, but for most it is nothing more than the only means of transportation to Rafiki's Planet Watch. Along the way, you get to see a few behind the scenes areas, but it's nothing too special in all reality. You can see some of the nighttime housing areas for some of the animals that are on stage each day and a guide points your attention towards the locations. For this train ride, it's more about the destination rather than the journey. As I mentioned earlier, this is also the train that passes Harambe Market and really completes the theming of that area as well. Overall, the Wildlife Express Train is a great tie in to increase the theming and overall experience of other areas of the park.

RAFIKI'S PLANET WATCH: The Planet Watch section of the park isn't too terribly exciting, but it is something you may want to look into if you have never done it before. While there are no actual attractions in the area, there are various learning experiences and it gives you a behind the scenes look at some of the animal services provided at Animal Kingdom. For example, in the event of natural disasters and other weather related phenomenons, Animal Kingdom and Epcot have used their unique facilities to recuperate sea turtles and other animals to a point at which they are able to return to the wild.

Often throughout these processes, you are able to witness the work being done to assist animals, but there are various veterinary services being performed year round. Despite being able to see the work being done to help, you can also learn about and interact with many animals as well. Although it isn't something you're likely to do every time you go into the park, it is a fairly unique opportunity that is very different from anything you will be able to experience anywhere else.

Habitat Habit!- On the path leading to the main Conservation Station area, there is a fun little experience where you can learn about and view Cotton-top Tamarin monkeys. Despite the strange name of this opportunity, it is fairly entertaining to see the monkeys, but you can always see a larger monkey display in the Asia portion of the park. If you're not too picky about what type of monkeys you are looking to see, then you can probably bypass this area of Rafiki's Planet Watch.

Conservation Station- As the main draw to Planet Watch, if you enjoy animals and learning about various types of animals, you will really enjoy the Conservation Station. The area isn't too large, but it is a fairly interactive walk through learning environment, which many guests enjoy. On select days, as you tour the exhibits, you may get to observe common medical treatments being performed on the animals under Disney's care. There are some hands-on activities as well, but the real benefit is the fact that most of the time the crowds aren't too overwhelming. It often gives you a good place to get away from some of the crowds for a while and enjoy something a little out of the ordinary for a theme park destination. Unfortunately, you do have to manage your expectations. The Conservation Station is definitely not a grand, large-scale attraction, but more of a small and creative opportunity to learn about the world around you.

Affection Section- Basically, Affection Section is a glorified petting zoo. As disappointing as that sounds, it is actually one of the better petting zoos I've seen. While I haven't actually experienced it in many years, due to various family allergies and rare trips to Rafiki's Planet Watch, it has never really been disappointing. Most of the animals are fairly ordinary, but a few are actually endangered or semi-endangered and under Disney's exclusive care. It's a great place to actually get to interact with the animals rather than just observe them moving about. Kids usually really enjoy the experience, and it makes for a fun little journey away from the main sections of the park.

Before moving on, I have to add something that often confuses many guests. Although it seems fairly self explanatory, the only way back to the rest of the park is on the same train you rode to Rafiki's Planet Watch in the first place. Sometimes this can be a little strange to some guests, but once you do it once, it makes a whole lot more sense after that. The train actually runs in a circle, so you see the first half on the way to Planet Watch and the second half on the way back to the original station.

ASIA: While I have never spent too much time in Asia at this park due to the fact that I have never really enjoyed Expedition Everest or been in the mood to get completely drenched at Kali River Rapids, it really does have a lot to offer. As the largest section of the park geographically, there is a good variety of family attractions and more intense offerings. In addition, Asia features some of the most creative theming aspects out of all the Disney parks.

If you're here for the attractions or just a quick walkthrough, be sure to take a minute to look around and take in all the little details and efforts made to develop an authentic experience. Over the past ten years, Asia has developed from an area with only one main attraction into arguably the most popular section of the park. Expedition Everest really pushed the area into a new era of design and moved the entire park into a new theming outlook. Today, that basis of theming is helping to push the park forward into an all day, all inclusive, Animal Kingdom which Disney has been searching for.

While it can be confusing getting to all of the attractions throughout Asia, the trick is that there are three ways of getting there. My best advice to find what you're looking for is that if you can't find something, just keep walking around the edge of the water, and you'll probably end up where you want to go. Pay attention to the place where you entered and the direction you are going by using the park map, and you will most likely have very few issues finding what you are looking for. As always, if you can't find something, flag down a cast member and I'm sure they will be happy to help. You never know, getting lost may create one of those great interactions with cast members that Disney has become synonymous with. Disney seems to have a special ability to make memories out of some of the most unexpected scenarios. It's great to hear about and even better to experience for yourself. No matter what the purpose of your vacation, I can guarantee that you will meet at least one cast member that goes above and beyond and gives you that one story you will want to share with anyone considering a Disney vacation.

Flights of Wonder- Even though the concept of the show is quite similar to the little pop up show I mentioned earlier, Flights of Wonder is a little more elaborate. The theatre is designed to look like one of the semi permanent locations found throughout Asia. However, seating has been fitted to the set up and offers a fairly large area for guests to sit and observe the many elements of the show. Most of the show is used to exhibit the many talents and personalities of various bird species, but there are also a few educational moments along the way. Surprisingly, there is a lot to learn and witness about birds that so many people overlook. Through flight demonstrations, it becomes obvious that many of the birds are underestimated in their immense capabilities.

For most people, this is a fun little show, but if you have any fear of birds, you should definitely sit this one out. If birds don't really sound all that interesting to you, still be sure to take about 25 minutes out of your day in the park to witness some of the many talents exhibited throughout Flights of Wonder. Once the birds fly over your head and perform variations of their wilderness behaviors, you may have a newly found respect for the creatures and potentially even a new favorite show in Animal Kingdom. It truly is an experience that is hard to match and great to see for yourself.

Yak and Yeti- While home to three different dining types, Yak and Yeti has a little something for everyone. Whether you want something quick for a counter service option, a drink to sit outside and enjoy, or a sit down meal with reservations available, it can all be found at this one location. Inside, and throughout the entire venue, there is a common theme.

While fairly simplistic, the theme is implemented in a very unique way. The restaurants involved with the Yak and Yeti name are all based off of the main concept of a travel lodge that you would stumble upon during a great journey across Asia. As fitting as it is, the restaurants sit at the base of the paramount adventure of the world, Mount Everest. Throughout the restaurant, you can easily see the many design elements that come from the Asian culture. Everything is intricately detailed, but also extremely simple in nature. There are no big signs that scream, "You are in Asia!", but the little details set the stage for a unique experience.

The location is clever in design and unique to the area, but the food is also set apart from the more traditional menu items of most theme parks. While it cannot be regarded as completely authentic Asian cuisine, the table service location features a menu of diverse semi-Asian offerings. It is a fairly creative menu, so some picky eaters will find it tough to find a menu item they will be happy with. But, if you're willing to branch out a little, most people find the items quite enjoyable. Moving on to the less elaborate part of Yak and Yeti, we come to the menu found at the Local Food Cafe portion of the location. As the counter service option, the food is a little less adventurous and focuses more on modernized Asian cuisine rather than the more authentic dishes found inside. At a much lower price point, this outdoor only area is a great option for a taste of the local eats, but at a price that makes them a little more enjoyable.

Lastly, we have the bar section of Yak and Yeti, but it really isn't the best bar available. The choices are limited and the window itself is just a branch off of the walk up counter service option. While Yak and Yeti is a great dining option while you are in Animal Kingdom, I cannot really recommend it for your ultimate counter service or table service choice. At Tusker House, you usually get a lot more for your money and the counter service is definitely no better than Flame Tree or Pizzafari. There are so many familiar options in the park that unless you are looking for something special and different, I really wouldn't recommend risking a dining plan credit or other means of payment on any aspect of the Yak and Yeti location. If you're an adventurous adult, go for it, but if not, you will probably want to look for a different option.

Maharajah Jungle Trek- It's hard for me to understand sometimes how Disney has never thought of a better, more immersive, experience than the jungle treks. As I said earlier, you basically just walk through at your own pace and look at animals. How is that different than a zoo? I know Disney could have developed a much better experience than they did. Why can't we take an ATV journey across the exhibits or float through them in a little boat ride? It doesn't make sense to me that a majority of the park is a glorified zoo. Maybe that's why I don't really enjoy Animal Kingdom as much as other guests do on a daily basis.

As mixed as my feelings are about the trails, I have to admit, the animals on the Maharajah Trek are the most interesting out of the four total trails. Most of the time, you can see a few Gibbons (monkeys) or some tigers that are fairly interesting and fun to watch for a little while, but as always, the trek lacks substance. You seem to walk very far for very little enjoyment. There is a variety of animals scattered about, but personally, I can't help but think your time can be spent elsewhere in the park or exploring the other parks to a greater extent.

Kali River Rapids- As the only true family boat ride in the four Florida parks, with the exception of Splash Mountain, Disney had to go big or go home with Kali River Rapids. As one of the few legit attractions in Animal Kingdom, Imagineering took the opportunity to make something memorable. Surprisingly the memories don't always come from the attraction itself, but rather as a result of what the attraction creates. What I mean by that is that most of the stories that come out of Kali River Rapids are more about how wet you got on the attraction rather than what the experience was actually like.

Getting off of Kali River Rapids has to go in its own category for getting off an attraction "wet". A better word to describe your status after the ride would be drenched, or maybe looking like you just walked through a hurricane. As much as an overreaction as that sounds, I guarantee it's the truth. If you're on the wrong side of the boat, you will not get off with a dry spot on you, but if you happen to be on the good side, it's a completely different story. On that side, you may get off primarily dry. So, I know what you're saying, "Simple enough, I'll just sit on the dry side of the boat!" As simple as that sounds, it's virtually impossible to predict due to the fact that the boat is circular and rotates constantly throughout your journey through the forest. So, long story short, if you don't want to get wet, do not get on Kali River Rapids! If you don't mind the moisture factor, it truly is a great attraction for all ages. It definitely will create a few lasting memories and good stories, but some people really don't like getting wet. Ride at your own risk, and be prepared to spend the next few hours a little more than damp if luck isn't on your side.

Mr. Kamal's- Kamal's has changed it's menu a few times, but today, it has it's most elaborate yet. Originally, it featured some boneless wing offerings, but now it has transitioned into a location that serves more intricate and authentic Asian food. Surprisingly, quite a few of these items are suitable for vegetarians, but also enjoyable for anyone else who may want to try them. Disney seems to be making a particular effort to cater to some of the more diet conscious people and has begun offering similar locations to this one across a majority of their parks. While it isn't much, it is a great option for some guests that have dietary restrictions or lifestyle choices that Disney can easily accommodate. Disney gets a lot of things right, and food is definitely a strong point in their guest service platform. Mr. Kamal's is a great example of that commitment to excellent service.

Warung Outpost- If you don't quite recognize that name, Upcountry may be a little more familiar to the returning guest. The name was changed a little while back, but the menu remained fairly similar. The Outpost is another little stand with some adult beverage choices that have a few creative names fitting the theme of the area. If you need a snack, you can get that here as well. Just like Mr. Kamal's, don't expect much. But, expect even less at Warung Outpost. The only comment I have to make here is that the amount of alcohol found in Animal Kingdom is a little outrageous. I understand some people really enjoy it, and I don't have a problem with that, but the parks never served alcohol until more recently in the scope of Disney history, and Disneyland still rarely sells alcohol outside of Club 33.

It seems strange to me, but also not strange at all that the only parks that serve mass amounts of alcohol are the ones Walt Disney himself had very little influence on. Shouldn't that hold some kind of precedent for the rest of the parks? His legacy should be kept in the highest regard possible, and if alcohol wasn't in the original park, I don't quite understand why it should be so incredibly prevalent in the newer parks. I have absolutely nothing against alcohol, but there had to be a reason for the decision in the first place, and it's hard to see the growing trend away from that original idea.

It really makes you think about what Walt Disney would think about the parks if he could walk through the gates today. With the exception of a majority of Disneyland, nearly everything has changed sense the building process began. Everything is modernized and monetary gains are becoming a main leading aspect of the company. It's extremely hard to believe that the magic of the parks could be getting lost in the desires of modern society. Magic used to be in the form of simple animatronics that were poised to change the world and that inspired future generations, but today that doesn't seem to be enough. There's something special about Disney for sure, but sadly, it doesn't seem to be invention and creativity, but rather details that bring the parks to life. Walt Disney World is undoubtedly growing, but it's hard not to look back at how it used used to be and not dream about how wonderful it must have been.

Anandapur Ice Cream Truck- Anandapur is just as it sounds, but so much more than you expect in person. It truly is an ice cream truck, but built into a modern day walk up window. What makes it special is the design and elaborate decoration across the truck itself. While it's still just an ice cream truck, the theming really fits the area and helps immerse you, as the guest, in a truly special environment. The food offerings are simple, just like the overlying concept. All they serve is soft serve ice cream and drinks of the non-alcoholic variety. It isn't much in the way of food, but it's one of those little details that really pulls all of the design aspects together.

Expedition Everest- Legend of the Forbidden Mountain- As the crown jewel of the park, Expedition Everest can be seen for miles. The mountain peeks far above any other point in the park, and seems to call people in. The Imagineers went above and beyond to create an incredibly intense journey that starts even at the base of the mountain. The queue for the attraction is a museum of the legend of the Yeti, and does an excellent job of explaining the story and setting the scene for one of the greatest developments in Disney history. The attraction took years to complete, but the result was well worth the wait. The recreation is nearly as majestic as the original mountain, which is a feat that is incredibly hard to imagine.

After you get past the story and are ready to conquer the monster himself, board the train and get ready for an adventure. While Disney tends to advertise the attraction as family friendly, don't be fooled. In reality, this is a proper thrill ride. Most people get off of the attraction the first time completely shocked, but ultimately amazed. The experience is honestly like no other and incredibly hard to explain without witnessing for yourself. The drop, which you can see before boarding, is only part of the thrill inducing equation. The coaster features a seemingly never ending corner and even a section in which the train reaches significant speed moving backwards along the track. As you can imagine, if you get motion sick, you do not want to be on this attraction!

As it is the most popular Disney mountain, be sure to get there early in the morning or utilize a fastpass+ to minimize wait times. As a sort of exception to my wait time rule of always passing on any wait that is over 45 minutes, Expedition Everest has to be experienced at least once while utilizing the standby queue. The queue really delivers the backstory and makes the experience that much more enjoyable.

While not being able to have the full fledge experience, you can really enjoy part of what Everest has to offer from the ground, just as you can the real mountain. The artistic ability put into the construction is incredibly awe inspiring. It truly is hard to believe that the structure is man made. The entire attraction is surrounded by trees and enveloped in elevation changes that are not so common to central Florida. Up close the details are obvious, but from a distance the whole picture really comes into play and creates that unsurpassable wow factor that shows all that Disney can be and ensures confidence in the new additions to the park.

After your journey, be sure to take a look around at Serka Zong Bazaar. The items here feature various Expedition Everest influences, but ultimately is a great place just to look around and find something special. It is the only true merchandise location in the Asia section of the park, so you won't want to miss what it has to offer before moving on. The merchandise is unique and a majority of it cannot be found at other merchandise locations.

DINOLAND U.S.A.: In my own personal opinion, I would save DinoLand for last. The reason for that is simple. At this point in the day, you have probably walked all across Animal Kingdom and really don't feel like walking anymore.

DinoLand is a great fix to that issue, due to the fact that nearly all of the attractions are very close together. In a park with very few real attractions, it is a welcomed change late in the day. There are more attractions in this little area than there are in virtually the entire park. DinoLand is sort of the exact opposite of the rest of Animal Kingdom. It's bold, colorful, "future focused", and surprisingly really enjoyable to wander around. With the creative expansions coming to Animal Kingdom, I can only image DinoLand lit up at night with all the neon lights and signs. Unfortunately, I have never had the opportunity to see the full extent of the nighttime environment, but it has to be a wonderful sight.

The Boneyard- It's hard to think about Dinosaurs without thinking about extinction and fossils. The Boneyard lets kids explore simulated fossil remains while having fun on an elaborate and expansive playground. Due to the fact that you can actually dig for bones, sections of the area are covered in sand and you will inevitably end up covered in it one way or another. With that reality in mind, it is a great place to get away from the crowded parks for a little while and let the kids run around and play. Surprisingly, it's a very similar set up to the recently closed Honey I Shrunk the Kids Playground at Hollywood Studios, but with much different theming. The biggest difference here is that a majority of the area is actually set up to accommodate adults, as well as kids. Many of the main parts of the playground have taller openings and walk ways that let the kids at heart explore the area as well. It's very difficult to find a playground this expansive and elaborately themed anywhere else. Try to put the sand out of mind for a little while and enjoy all the Boneyard has to offer for guests of all ages.

TriceraTop Spin- In the center of DinoLand is this simple, but enjoyable attraction which is very similar to Dumbo. TriceraTop Spin has never been quite as popular as Dumbo, so if your child isn't caught up in the theming, as most kids aren't, TriceraTop Spin is a great alternative. Despite not being quite as grand and elaborate as the flying elephants, the overall experience is pretty much the same. A couple people get in a dinosaur, instead of an elephant, and you make it go up and down as the entire group of vehicles spin. While it's basically the same design, most of the time, you will hardly ever wait more then 20 minutes to ride TriceraTop Spin, where as Dumbo nearly always has a 45+ minute wait time. The nostalgia factor isn't really present, which is probably the reason for the shorter lines, but some people really don't care about the history of an attraction. If you're one of those people, skip Dumbo and ride some dinosaurs instead!

Fossil Fun Games- These games are probably one of the only things in Animal Kingdom I have an actual issue with. They're carnival style games similar to Whack-a-Mole and so on, but you actually have to pay to play them. As usual, if you win, you get a prize, but if you're paying 100 dollars to get in a park, all of the attractions better be free. Due to other people assumably in the same mindset, hardly any guests ever pay the price to play. It really isn't worth it, and your time can be spent in better ways. You can play carnival games at your local fair, so why waste your time playing them at Disney World? Other than the fact that the Fossil Fun Games help further develop the theming as a bright, charismatic area, they aren't games that are special or unique and can ultimately be skipped over completely.

Restaurantosaurus- In the past, this dining location was one of the few restaurants in Walt Disney World where you could actually get Mcdonald's menu items. It wasn't exactly the same, but they had most of the items you would want to purchase. After Disney removed McDonald's from the parks a few years ago, Restaurantosaurus developed into what it is today.

The newer menu is based on strictly American food that includes hotdogs, cheeseburgers, and a few other options that are all pretty enjoyable while being very simple. The theming of the area, as with most Disney counter service meals, is what really makes the meal enjoyable and a must do for quite a few guests. Even before you enter the building, the entire exterior has the humorous appearance of a hodgepodge, thrown together compilation of various buildings and trailers that you can't help but smile when you see. The interior is no different, Dinosaur inspired artwork covers the walls and humorous references are scattered throughout the theming as well. Since the entire restaurant is sort of a compilation of various buildings thrown together to establish an intriguing theme, there is always ample seating available for even the most crowded days in the parks. On top of that, the building is air conditioned and in Animal Kingdom, trust me, you'll need it.

Although the food isn't extravagant, and the atmosphere is intended to come off as sort of a big joke, it makes dining at Restaurantosaurus an incredibly entertaining part of a day at Animal Kingdom. Some people miss the McDonald's food, but personally, I'm glad that some of the corporate brands are leaving the parks with the recent Disney push to get more name brand items into the parks. I have never really liked it when Disney outsourced food, but it's great to see them developing their own menus at least at this one location.

DINOSAUR- While most attractions at Walt Disney World are suited for kids, DINOSAUR really isn't (despite what Disney claims). The entire attraction is based on the concept of going back in time in your ride vehicle, called a Time Rover, to capture a special dinosaur and save it from extinction. The entire mission is under a time constraint in order to avoid the meteor shower that wiped out the dinosaur population. As you can imagine, the mission doesn't go as planned, and as you travel through the past, you are confronted by many larger than life animatronic dinosaurs that threatened to end the journey prematurely.

The dinosaurs are incredibly loud and are often quite scary to young children, but on top of that, the attraction is incredibly jerky and not suited for other types of guests as well. If you get motion sick, do not get on DINOSAUR! I made that mistake once and felt terrible for hours after, and that's coming from someone who has been on both Space Mountain and Expedition Everest with virtually no problems.

If you're someone who doesn't fit either of those categories that may experience problems, it can actually be a very entertaining journey. Most people laugh and scream and enjoy the various twists and turns of the Time Rover, but it definitely isn't always a family friendly attraction. Once you get off, be sure to look at the picture that is taken during the ride. Nearly every time, someone in your family will have a look on their face that will be priceless and memorable for years to come. DINOSAUR can be a very entertaining attraction, but as with any ride, know your limits in order to really enjoy your time in the parks.

The Dino Institute Shop- The shop is set up as the gift shop for Dino Institute which plays a role in the theming of the DINOSAUR attraction. This is where you can purchase your on-ride picture, but also one of the only merchandise locations devoted solely to dinosaur merchandise. It is actually a very large shop, so if you decide not to ride DINOSAUR, you can look around in here for a little while and keep yourself occupied. There's a lot to look at, and you never know when you'll find that one special souvenir item that sparks your interest.

Dino-Bite Snacks- I'm not quite sure if the play on words was intentional or not, but the desserts here definitely don't disappoint. The location is right at the end of Restaurantosaurus and fairly easy to miss. But, if you're looking for good desserts, you'll want to take the time to find it. They have a limited menu, but a very good menu. Dino-Bite Snacks serves Häagen-Dazs ice-cream and a few other dessert items. But, in a park with very few dessert offerings, Dino-Bite Snacks is pretty hard to pass up. Whatever you decide to order will be enjoyable, but the downfall of the location is that unless you decide to eat in Restaurantosaurus, this counter service location has no seating area of it's own.

Trilo-Bites- For many years, Trilo-Bites was the home of the iconic Disney turkey legs that so many guests love. For some reason, unknown to me, Disney decided to change the menu, and I'm not positive it was for the better. Ultimately, they turned Trilo-Bites into a snack only dining location. The new menu is based on three strange items: a waffle sundae, a buffalo chicken waffle slider, and a variety of ice cream floats. There is nothing particularly wrong with the limited offerings, but it is a little strange for Disney to replace a park icon with a menu item that appeals to as limited of an audience as buffalo chicken waffle sliders do. With that weird menu change, I would recommend moving on to either Restaurantosaurus or Flame Tree Barbecue, which are both nearby.

Primeval Whirl- While this little rollercoaster is far from a thrill ride, it is a great family coaster. The goal of the attraction is to vaguely simulate a journey back in time, but the theming is pretty simple. The ride vehicle is probably the most interesting and thrilling part of the entire attraction. The seating within the vehicle is set up in a way that each guest sits in a circular pattern with an open front to see where you're going. Once the attraction reaches a certain point on the track, the vehicle begins to spin freely and it really adds to the overall experience. The spinning isn't enough to make most people nauseous and actually is a clever part of the design. After the spinning begins, the ride vehicle freely rotates for the rest of the attraction as it goes up and down hills. The first time you try it, it can be a little disorienting, but you can't help but laugh the whole time and leave with a big smile on your face.

I do have to finish with a few words of caution. The spinning can bother more sensitive guests and those with motion sickness really shouldn't ride Primeval Whirl. In addition, probably due to the ride vehicle design, the height requirement is one of the tallest I have ever seen. At a 48 inch requirement, it is an even higher requirement than Expedition Everest. If you have a shorter guest in your group or young children, be sure to check their height before getting them too interested in the attraction. I have seen far too many sad faces turned away from Primeval Whirl, and that's never something you want to see at the happiest place on earth!

Chester and Hester's Dinosaur Treasures- Chester and Hester really made this store into something special. While the two are assumedly fictional characters, their store is one of the more interesting to look around in due to the wonderful environment. Once you walk in the door, you go into sensory overload. There's merchandise everywhere, things hanging from the ceiling and various model trains circling the room. You could quite literally go in the store 100 times and never see everything that is on the walls. Somehow, this scattered theming really plays into the overall merchandise sold. They sell a little bit of everything, but primarily toys and stuffed animals. It's everything most kids love. There's loud noises, a lot going on around the room, and toys and souvenirs all over the place. I walked by the store for years assuming it was just another Disney gift shop, but once you see it for the first time, it's hard not to want stop in every time you're close by.

Dino Diner- This little stand is far from an actual diner, so don't expect too much. The so called "diner" is just a little trailer that serves food out of one side. It's pretty obvious that the trailer design is intentional, but I couldn't imagine why. If you can get past the fact that it really isn't a diner at all, the food offerings are a little creative and fit the semi make shift carnival atmosphere. All you can get from the stand is glazed nuts, beer, and a few other snack items. Don't expect much, but it is a pretty good place to use a snack credit on the Disney Dining Plan.

Finding Nemo - The Musical- In the opinion of some guests, I have saved the best for last. In my opinion, Festival of The Lion King is a much better show, but many guests prefer the elaborate production found at Finding Nemo - The Musical. Quite a few years ago, the stage for this show was used as a Tarzan themed experience called Tarzan Rocks! At the time, it was one of my favorite experiences in the park and probably would still be today. The production included high flying stunts on roller-skates, great music, and even a little bit of audience interaction. But, for one reason or another, Disney decided that it needed to go. Finding Nemo was its eventual replacement.

Although I am a little biased because of what the attraction used to be, I have to admit that the Nemo musical is one of the best I have ever seen. The show is fairly clever in design and does a great job of keeping the audience involved no matter what their interest is in the original movie. For example, the actors on stage control various puppets that are incredibly detailed and complicated to control properly. Just watching how skilled the performers are while singing and dancing on stage is entertaining in and of itself. On top of that, you have to be amazed by the parts of the show which swing the actors out over the crowd and around the room. To be honest, I don't really enjoy the music, but I do really enjoy watching the various puppets in action. Although, if you do love a good catchy song, the musical won't let you down with songs developed by Broadway level musicians. For the music enthusiast, it doesn't stop there. All of the performers on stage are actually singing the music live and are incredibly talented. So, if musicals are your thing or if you really don't appreciate them at all, there is something for everyone to be entertained by at the Finding Nemo musical.

As you can probably tell, Animal Kingdom is most definitely not my favorite park, and I really just figured out why while writing about each and every attraction. There is nearly no connection to Walt Disney or his vision for the parks. I completely understand that he had no serious involvement with Animal Kingdom, if any at all, but it's hard to connect with the experience when the history just isn't there. I've always wanted it to develop into something special, but it doesn't have that wow factor. Each of the other parks have something that continually draws guests back or something that makes them never want to leave. In the case of Animal Kingdom, it really isn't all that hard to find a reason to leave the park.

I couldn't use the word magical to describe more than maybe three attractions throughout Animal Kingdom. With the exceptions of Expedition Everest, Kilimanjaro Safaris, and potentially Festival of the Lion King, there really isn't that wow factor in the park that most people come to Disney to experience. For most people, there are no childhood memories wandering through the streets of Animal Kingdom and no stories to be told as a result. When the other parks have such a rich history and story of their own to tell, Animal Kingdom seems to have gotten lost along the way. Part of that has to be linked to Animal Kingdom being the newest of the four parks, but hopefully those connections and stories will develop over time. With so many wonderful experiences at Walt Disney World, if you were ever put into a situation where you had three days to see three parks, I wouldn't hesitate to tell you to skip Animal Kingdom. It would be a wonderful place to visit if it was on its own anywhere else in the world, but it doesn't measure up to the rest of the parks at the Walt Disney World Resort at this time.

Although it is obvious that I have mixed feelings about Animal Kingdom, I would be going against my own thought process if I finished off this section here. I always have to remind myself that the reason we go to Walt Disney World isn't for the parks and the attractions or even all the wonderful things those experiences create. We go to the parks to create memories and to remember what it's like to be a kid again. Nobody ever wants to grow up, and Disney gives each and every one of us that unique and wonderful sensation of being a kid again. Sure, there is a lot of things I really don't care for at Walt Disney World, but I will never stop going to the parks. There's no better feeling than creating a memory that you know you will have for the rest of your life. The stories from our various childhood memories come to life right before our eyes in the parks and allow us to create new stories with those around us.

I wrote this book to help people escape reality for a little while and plan for the adventure of a lifetime. I never thought the book would give me something in return, but as I wrote, I was able to reflect upon and appreciate all of the opportunities the parks have provided for me over the years. Disney gave me a hobby, a stack of memories that could never be counted, and if this book does well, potentially a future doing what I love to do. Ultimately, it's not about the numbers or even my future, but helping people experience for themselves the joy and amusement the parks have given me over the years. Hopefully, by giving a little description of all aspects of Disney World, you can pick and choose what is going to provide for you and your family the adventure of a lifetime!

YOUR HIGHWAY IN THE SKY!

I'll get straight to the point, the monorail system at Walt Disney World is one of the most overlooked, but incredibly helpful parts of Walt Disney World. Most people use the express monorails to get to and from the Magic Kingdom (even though they shouldn't, but we'll get to that later) and that's it! In my opinion, if at the end of a week long vacation, you can't quote at least one of the monorail monologues, then you're doing something wrong, especially if you're staying at one of the resorts on the Magic Kingdom loop. The monorails can be used for so many wonderful things and are unlike any sort of transportation you have ever experienced before. They're incredibly efficient and distinctly Disney. So, under the understanding that you can never use the monorails too much, here are my top tips for utilizing all the highway in the sky has to offer with a little history thrown in the mix.

-We have to start off with the simplest tip I can give. Use the Monorail to get to Epcot if you can! If you are at any monorail station, you can travel to Epcot by way of the monorail. Board the resort loop at any stop, then get off at the Transportation and Ticket Center. Simply walk down one ramp and up another, and you will be on your way to Epcot once you board a second "train". To get back to your resort or the Magic Kingdom, do the same thing in reverse. Using the monorail rather than the buses will save you an incredible amount of time and effort, especially at park closing times.

-If this book ever becomes semi-popular, I'll regret ever saying this. But, instead of going straight to the express monorail when you park at the Ticket and Transportation Center, board the resort monorail. I have been using this tip for years, and I have never had an issue. Many guests assume that the resort monorail only stops at the resorts, but that is not the case at all. With the exception of the Epcot loop, all of the monorails eventually end up at Magic Kingdom. On a recent trip on New Years Eve, I used this trick and bypassed a wait of over 200 people in the express line and got in line behind 4 guests in the resort loop waiting area instead.

-*Monorail History:* The original route simply circled the lake in front of the Magic Kingdom. The Epcot loop was added years later and expanded the system. What many people don't know is that there were plans rumored over the years that the monorail was always designed to be

155

extended to other parts of the Disney property, but it was never accomplished.

-If you're ever looking for something relatively cheap and incredibly fun to do, try resort hopping on the Magic Kingdom loop. You never have to pay to ride the monorail, and you can always avoid the cost of spending a day in the parks to relax and enjoy all the resorts have to offer. You can eat at any of the properties, no matter if you have a park ticket for the day or not. Even on the dining plan, your meals are linked to your rooming accommodations rather than your days in the parks. The resorts are home to some of the best dining experiences on property and so many people overlook resort dining altogether. Between meals or snacks, feel free to wander the resorts and look at the various gift shops, relax in some of the hammocks, or even lounge around in the lobby. Disney doesn't mind, because they understand you may be a potential buyer and return to the resort later as a paying guest. Either way, they make money off of you in some way or another through food, merchandise, or even free advertising by word of mouth. The only restrictions they are beginning to put into place is that you are no longer allowed to use the resort pools at many locations without room key access. Very few guests were doing this, but it is completely understandable why Disney would want to reserve that privilege to resort guests only.

-At any of the monorail resort stops, you can take boats to other resorts, as well as the Magic Kingdom. Similar to the resort hopping on the monorail, you can do the same thing with the boats, but it is a little more complicated. Your simplest option is to board a boat to Fort Wilderness, Wilderness Lodge, or the Contemporary, then get on the boat that is exclusively for the resorts from one of those docks. Many people don't realize you can get to Wilderness Lodge and the campgrounds fairly easily from the Magic Kingdom, and by figuring that out, you open yourself up to a few more dining locations when you can't find a reservation or don't wish to eat in the park. When you're done with your free voyages across the lake, board a monorail at Magic Kingdom, the Contemporary, the Polynesian Village, or even the Grand Floridian, and you can get back to where you began with ease.

-*Monorail History:* When the monorail concept was first developed it was designed to be a sustainable and eco friendly system of transportation before anyone worried about being eco friendly. The entire system has run on electricity and has been incredibly efficient for over 30 years!

-Always use the monorails instead of the ferry boats to get to the Magic Kingdom. The ferry boats take forever and they are always overcrowded and really aren't very enjoyable to ride.

-When you are boarding a monorail at any of the various stations, never try to board right in the middle. Walk a little farther to one end or the other and you will usually find a completely empty or near empty car. Take your time, and don't worry about running to find a seat. The monorails are nothing like the shuttles at the airports and are actually driven by cast members that will never leave without every guest safely on board or behind the designated waiting gate.

-If you miss a monorail, don't panic. Usually within 5-10 minutes, another monorail will be at your station and ready to board.

As you can clearly see, there are an incredible amount of benefits and extra opportunities when you utilize the monorails effectively. It doesn't hurt that they are really fun to ride as well! You can see so much as you travel high in the air around the Seven Seas Lagoon that you really can't witness through the windows of a car or bus. The whole experience is memorable and does an excellent job of bringing families together both literally and metaphorically.

Monorails really bring people together in a weird way. As soon as you step inside, people start to open up. You can have great conversations with complete strangers and for some reason, it doesn't seem strange at all. Everyone is having a great time and you're all happy to be there. That happiness is one of those things that really makes Disney special. No matter how long your day was or how exhausted you are, you can always look around you and find that one person with a big smile on their face. It's these simple moments that make a Disney Vacation worth the time and money you put into it.

Disney was built on the simple idea of making people laugh and smile together. Thankfully, that goal will always be achievable at Walt Disney World. You don't have to be having a great day to have the time of your life at any of the Disney parks. It could rain all day, and I guarantee you will still have an incredible experience. It's genuinely amazing how those memories unfold so effortlessly throughout every guests' time in the parks. I've never worked for Disney, so nobody is paying me to say that, but I promise you every word of it is true. I have been blessed to have the opportunity to go to the parks many times throughout my life, and I have a stack of memories as a result that is taller than I could have ever imagined.

THE DISNEY DINING PLAN

Dining at Disney can be extremely expensive, and is a hidden cost that most guests tend to overlook on their first trip to the parks. The Disney Dining Plan gives every guest the opportunity to pay for their meals before their vacation, if they wish to do so. When you pay in advance, it gives you a much better idea of what you will be spending in total on your Disney vacation. The service is offered exclusively to resort guests and is one of the many benefits of staying on property.

The cost of the plan is around $60 per person per day of your resort stay. For children under the age of nine, the cost is much lower at $20 per child per day. The regular dining plan gives each guest the option of a table service meal, a counter service meal, and a snack item for each day of their vacation. There is a higher priced plan available with more meals per day as well as a lower priced plan with exclusively quick service meals. Although the other plans are offered, the only way you can really get your moneys worth out of the dining plan is to get the regular version. By the time you eat a table service meal, a counter service meal, and a snack item, you will be beyond full the entire day.

-Above: Family Style Breakfast at Whispering Canyon

When you break down the cost of each item included in the plan, then compare it to the cost you would be paying out of pocket, you do save a little bit of money. While this sounds good in theory, it really isn't as good of a deal as Disney wants you to believe it is. By the time most guests eat a table service meal, which includes buffets, they typically won't eat but one other meal or snack the rest of the day. On the dining plan, you are given both items and many days, the snack item or the second meal goes unused. The meals and snacks roll over to the next day, but, by the end of your stay, you have paid for a bunch of snacks that you would have never bought in the first place without the dining plan. Most people end up picking up a bunch of Mickey rice crispy treats to take home on the last day to get rid of the snack credits.

For most new guests, the terms used in this resort add on package are a little strange, so I will do my best to explain each item that is included with your purchase. The items included are as follows per guest per day of your stay:

1 TABLE SERVICE CREDIT- A table service credit is valid at nearly any of the sit-down restaurants at the Disney parks and resorts. For example, if you want to go to the Crystal Palace in Magic Kingdom, you would use one table service credit per person to pay for your meal. The only real issue you can face with the table service credits is that a few of the more high end offerings, such as the Yachtsman Steakhouse and Le Cellier, require two table service credits for one meal. In these unique circumstances, you have to skip a table service meal on another day or pick a different dining location. Personally, I would pick another dining location. While the high end restaurants are nice and the food is great, it isn't really worth sacrificing an additional dining experience or even a buffet to do so.

1 COUNTER SERVICE CREDIT- Counter service (also described as quick service) is basically the walk up windows and the fast food style restaurants. You walk up to the counter and order your food as opposed to having a server that takes your order and brings it to you. A majority of the counter service food gets extremely repetitive, so I advise that you use these credits at the world showcase locations or some of the other options that aren't just burgers and fries. If you eat burgers everyday, you end up having the same tasting Disney cheeseburger at virtually every location. Disney cheeseburgers are pretty good, but it definitely gets repetitive on a longer vacation.

1 SNACK ITEM- The snack items are probably the highlight of the dining plan. There are tons of snack options, and you can find them just about anywhere. Snacks range from baked goods to ice-cream and virtually everything in between. It's often nice to have a little treat sometime throughout the day or late at night as you leave the park.

However, this is the part of the plan that most people wouldn't necessarily buy every day. But, it is quite nice to know you can grab a snack at any time. Be on the lookout for great snack items. So many people use the credits for popsicles and simple food items, but they can actually be used for much better options. For example, at the ice cream parlor on Mainstream U.S.A., you can get a huge homemade ice-cream cookie sandwich for the exact same snack credit some people use for a pre packaged cookie at the Emporium. I know I would rather have the giant sandwich rather than a cookie that has probably been in the package for weeks!

One last thing to consider with these credits is that under the new dining plan restrictions, Disney has decided to allow virtually any single serving item to be categorized as a snack credit. The old plan for snacks was based on the price point of the item rather than what Disney considers a snack size portion. Surprisingly, with the recent change, there are a lot more snack items available under the dining plan, which makes it a much better value for your money. Now instead of having to buy breakfast with a drink and a side and a main item and use a counter service credit, you can choose to just buy one item and call it a snack credit in many cases. For example, say you get a scone or baked good of some sort at one of the various bakeries and call it breakfast for the day. It's a Disney vacation-eat cake for breakfast if you really want to! In either case, you can avoid using a table service credit and getting all of those extra items you may not want or need and use a snack credit instead.

1 REFILLABLE DRINK MUG- The refillable mugs are essentially souvenir drink cups that allow you to get unlimited refills at your designated resort. The part that trips most people up is that they cannot be used to get unlimited refills at the parks. For most guests, the refillable mugs aren't a must have item. Once again, if you paid for your food outright rather than on the dining plan, you would not include this expensive addition. I do have to say that during the summer or while spending some time at the resort pool, it is great to be able to walk inside and grab a "free" drink. Although at some resorts the pool isn't as convenient as it is at others. For resorts like the Wilderness Lodge, with a drink location a few steps from the pool, its hard to beat. At some of the All-Stars, the refillable mugs aren't as convenient and the same is true at many of the more spread out Moderates as well.

In the long run, if you plan on eating a lot during your stay and you're that guest that comes for the food more than the attractions, the dining plan will be a great fit. You pay for everything ahead of time and can sit back, relax, and eat all day. For most guests though, the dining plan is more of a convenience rather than a necessity. You are usually paying for something you don't really need or that you usually wouldn't eat in the first place. Disney does a great job of playing up the savings aspect of the program, but you have to credit them for making recent adjustments that favor the guest rather than their profit margin.

Starting in 2016, the dining plan has some new options and a greater degree of flexibility than it has in the past. For example, many guests would rather use a counter service meal as snack credits. Under the old plan, you couldn't really do that unless it was a special circumstance with an understanding cast member. Under the new system, you can easily use one counter service meal for three or less snack items. Essentially, you are getting the same use out of your payment, but you now have a greater control over what you're getting for your various credits. You can now get what you want rather than what Disney wants you to have. It's a great change and one that gives the guest many more options, but as with anything at Disney, these new options could change over night.

When buying into the dining plan, take into consideration what you're going to use, and purchase accordingly. If your vacation is for dining purposes mainly, go for it; it will turn out to be a great deal. You may even want to make the jump to the Deluxe Dining Plan which gives you a more exclusively upscale dining experience and more food than you could ever imagine. The dining plan works best for guests who want to know, down to the last cent, what their vacation will cost ahead of time, but for others it really isn't the best fit. No two guests are the same, so take some of this into consideration and pick the best fit for you.

FASTPASS+: A DEVELOPING IDEA

For years, fastpasses were incredibly simple and easy to use, but recently, Disney decided to change everything. In a claimed effort to more successfully control the constantly growing crowds, Disney came up with the fastpass+ system. The new system cost Disney an outrageous amount of money to develop and, in my opinion, it didn't live up to expectations, despite great intentions. It pretty much ended up being an online reservation service for attractions throughout the parks.

While the system is virtually guaranteed to change and develop in time, I'll do my best to explain the current process, due to the fact that it confuses so many first time guests. Right after you book your vacation, get ready to book your fastpass+ selections. Within 60 days of your checkin date, as a resort guest, you can book three attractions per day for which you will get a reserved time to enter a separate line and board the attraction under virtually no wait time. The problem that arises is that many of the more popular attractions are very difficult to get your desired fastpass+ selection preferences. For example, at the beginning of the time frame and often within the first few hours of availability, the Seven Dwarfs Mine Train will be booked solid. Occasionally, you will get lucky and find a fastpass+ that someone else dropped, but there is no guarantee. You can either keep checking and hope for the best, or book as early as you possibly can in hopes of securing the perfect fastpass+ options. Once you make your selections, they will appear on what Disney calls a Magic Band which functions as your park ticket, room key, and can even be used as a payment option similar to Apple Pay. The bands will most likely be delivered to your house, as long as you book far enough in advance. In some unique cases, they will be waiting for you when you arrive at resort check in.

The entire system is internet based and linked to a website and application called My Disney Experience. On your account, after reserving your resort room, you can book your fastpass selections quick and easy as well as your dining reservations. If for some reason you don't want to use the advanced selection options, you can always attempt to book your choices once you get to the park itself, but don't expect to get every attraction you are hoping for. Fastpasses are limited, as I mentioned before, and while cast members will do all they can to help you, if there are none left, there are none left. Also good to note here is that offsite guests utilizing the My Disney Experience system for Fastpass+ can only book selections for attractions 30 days prior to their stay and will have to purchase Magic Bands if they wish to use them. That's just one more benefit of staying on property!

As for the selection process itself, in Epcot and Hollywood Studios, you get to pick one of the more popular attractions and then two other, less popular attractions as well. However, in Magic Kingdom and Animal Kingdom, you get to choose any three attractions, no matter what the popularity of the attraction is. If it is available, you can book it. The most interesting part of the program is that once you use your three fastpasses for the day, you can book an additional fastpass by using one of the fastpass+ kiosks throughout the parks or the smart phone application. Many guests overlook this option, and if you are willing to stay late in the day, you can usually get another pass for something like Buzz Lightyear's Space Ranger Spin or even Pirates of the Caribbean.

If this is your first time hearing about the new system, I can imagine this is a bit confusing, but once you try it yourself, it is incredibly simple to understand. You may experience a little technology hiccup along the way, but simply call Disney and they will be happy to fix whatever problem you are experiencing. The first time you use the system, I would highly recommend utilizing the app that Disney has developed. The app is much more user friendly than the full fledge website, and the results are nearly identical. Additionally, never try to book fastpasses for a group of more than 8-10 people. It will be virtually impossible to keep track of everything and appease every member of your group. Lastly, I recommend that you use your fastpass+ selections to cover the three attractions that you decide you want to do more than anything else. If you do so, you are virtually guaranteed to get on those attractions and put a big smile on your families faces no matter what the rest of the day has in store.

Fastpasses used to be a paper based system that would do basically the same thing the electronic system does today. The big difference was that the old system allowed you to walk into the park and go get a fastpass for virtually any attraction. After you used that pass, you could easily get another one and there was no limit of how many you could use. Unfortunately, the system began to be less functional as the park attendance numbers rose and Disney decided to make a change at Walt Disney World. The paper system is still in place at Disneyland, but I do not believe it will ever return to Disney World. They have spent too much money to let it fail at this point. Originally, I had my hesitations about fastpass+, but it keeps getting more and more user friendly. I still miss the old fastpass kiosks and the paper tickets, but it is nice to be able to walk into the park knowing that you are guaranteed a ride on your favorite attraction. It's far from perfect, but ultimately, something that is here to stay. Disney will continue to fix the issues and hopefully, in time, My Disney Experience will live up to it's name and provide a great experience for each and every guest.

FINAL THOUGHTS

After returning from a Disney vacation, it will be obvious that this book could go on for hundreds of pages, but I really hope this short compilation helps you out in some way or another. I tried my best to include anything you would need to know about the parks, but still give you the opportunity to learn and explore certain aspects of the Disney experience for yourself. As I said when I started writing, you can't expect to see and do everything, but you will create memories that will last a lifetime. For quite some time, I didn't really understand why Disney's slogan for 2015-2016 was, "Unforgettable Happens Here", but while writing this book I finally figured it out. The moments in time you spend with friends and family doing something special is something you will never forget. Nearly every attraction in this book has some sort of wonderful memory of friends or family attached to it. It truly is unbelievable how much the parks have changed my life and continue to change the lives of people every single day. You can go to Disney and feel something you haven't felt since you were a kid. You can go and just have fun and not worry about anything else or about what anyone thinks about you.

Disney is the only place where a fully grown man can slap on some Mickey ears and nobody will take a second look. You're encouraged to have fun and to have the time of your life in whatever way you choose. No matter what situation or stage of life you're in, there is something at Walt Disney World that will make you feel like a kid in a candy store all over again. Ultimately, if you don't get anything else out of this book, realize one thing: there is something for everyone to enjoy. The Disney company owns a little bit of everything and finding what you love to do and doing it in the Disney mindset is something that can't be put into words. Sure, the parks will change and the experiences will change, but one thing is for sure: Disney will always be a place that allows each and every guest to create moments that take your breath away. Go to Disney, enjoy every moment, and remember, there is always a reason to return. It may not be the same when you get back, but you'll never regret coming back. The memories are never ending, and Disney keeps on giving. You never know, with the recent parks expansions and the great new films, you may be witnessing before your very eyes the next Disney Golden Age!

I'll leave you with one final thought. As you go through the parks, think about all the wonderful memories you've had in life. We don't remember what we were doing, how we got there, or where we spent the night before. We remember, more than anything, the people we were with. The stories come from the people, not the places or the things. We love it, not because of what the place is like, but because of what the place creates. Disney creates memories, and you can't put a price tag on a memory. Disney is an incredible story teller, but their greatest stories aren't the ones from the attractions or on-screen, but the stories guests tell from the experiences they've had in the parks, the memories that will last a lifetime!

In all reality, that has been the purpose of the parks from the beginning. Walt's vision was to create a place where families could have fun together and could create exciting memories rather than ones filled with dilapidated rides and sitting around watching kids have all the fun. He wanted people to feel like a kid again and to do so in a place that developed a lasting influence. He knew memories weren't made by the place, but rather that the place was instrumental in creating the memories. That's what the adventure is all about. You don't know what you'll find on your Disney vacation, but you can rest assured that you'll leave with something you never thought you would. It really is a special place, and I hope this guide is just a gateway to all the parks have in store for you. Thanks for reading, and enjoy your adventure at Walt Disney World!

MY GUARANTEE

I wouldn't have written this book if I didn't think it would be helpful, but to guarantee that I meet that goal, I will offer something a little extra special for anyone who chooses to utilize it. If you have any questions about the Disney parks and resorts, related or unrelated to anything in this book, feel free to email me at **theadventurersguide@yahoo.com**. I will do my best to answer each and every question in order for you to get the absolute most out of your adventure in the Disney parks.

SPECIAL THANKS

     "The Adventurer's Guide to Walt Disney World" is in no way affiliated with the Walt Disney Company. Disney retains all rights to the story elements of attractions and dining experiences, including menus. The writing in this book represents the ideas and opinions of the author. For official information about the Disney Parks reference their website by using the link provided below.

<u>https://disneyparks.disney.go.com</u>

The cover images belong to Trevor Aydelotte of Orlandobrothas. Be sure to take a look at all of his pictures on Instagram, Twitter, and Flickr. If you ever need any images of Walt Disney World or the Orlando area be sure to look him up. His work never disappoints!

     A special thanks also has to go out to all of my friends and family who have helped along the way. Without their support and encouragement, this book may have never become a reality. Family and friends are the key to the entire Disney adventure and I'm happy to say my family has helped me experience the adventure of a lifetime!

     Thank you to each and every reader. I hope this book will help you enjoy the parks for the very first time or let you experience them in a way you never thought you could before. If you have any unanswered questions, kind words, or press inquiries feel free to send me an email at **theadventurersguide@yahoo.com**. Thanks again, and enjoy the parks!

Follow the book on any of the following social media outlets and be sure to share with friends!

-Facebook: The Adventurer's Guide to Walt Disney World
-Twitter: @guide4disney

Official editing performed by: Caitlin Kendall

www.ingramcontent.com/pod-product-compliance
Lightning Source LLC
LaVergne TN
LVHW060026110325
805636LV00044B/1848